10 STEPS TO HERO

HOW TO CRAFT A KICKASS PROTAGONIST

SACHA BLACK

For all the writers who need a little dust on their halo.

READ ME FIRST

I started *13 Steps to Evil - How to Craft a Superbad Villain* by saying: 'heroes are interesting. But mostly they're predictable.' I wrote that book because I wanted to throw a Hiroshima-sized nuke into character creation, up the tension, build the villainous ante and slather stories with enough conflict and nail-biting action readers would rather eat their own kidney than put your books down. And it worked. Thousands of you bought and read *13 Steps to Evil* and developed your villains into sinister badasses.

But that also created a problem.

Your villains stole the limelight and your heroes were neglected, left in the dark — or maybe I should say light — to stare longingly at their glowingly heroic complexions as they decided which princess to save next. It's safe to say that, more often than not, heroes are dull and predictable. But they shouldn't be. And that's why I had to swallow my villainous love and write this book.

It's time to get down and dirty with your protagonist, dust off your star-spangled chivalry pants and prepare for hero beating (into shape, of course; not defeat. This is a book about heroes.

And I promise to stop the villain worship in a minute... probably).

This book will help you take your heroes from cardboard cut outs to dashing debonairs with glints in their eyes, dusty haloes and killer character arcs. Together, we're going to make sure the hero-charm doesn't flatten your story. We don't want heroes with sagging muscles like a has-been Olympic star, thank you very much. Instead, your hero will swoon his way into your readers' hearts and grip them page after page after page. Sound like the kind of awesome story with kickass characters you're after? Then I can help.

If you're reading this, my guess is you fit into one of the following categories:

- Your hero is flat, boring or not quite cutting it on the charisma scale
- You're a cape-wearing villain at heart and couldn't possibly write a charismatic, handsome hero
- You already wrote a hero, but they were clichéd and sporting an ego bigger than your word count
- You just want to write better characters

A few points to note about reading this book:
I've (where possible) avoided any duplication of content from *13 Steps to Evil*. Where you will inevitably see repetition is in the definition of a word or term. After all, things can only mean what they mean, and heroes and villains are essentially both 'book characters'. Therefore, there is some minor overlap.

I have used the words 'hero' and 'protagonist' interchangeably throughout this book to avoid repetitive word use. However, they do mean slightly different things in literary terms, and I'll explain the difference in *STEP 1 - Define the Debonair*. For clarity – use whichever word fits your character and your story.

I've used a wide range of well-known books and films as

examples throughout this book. I've stuck to well-known ones to minimize spoilers. But, inevitably, to illustrate an example fully I've had to explain some plots. You can avoid all spoilers by skipping over the examples.

But don't skip them. They're helpful, obviously.

If you're faint of heart, dislike bad words or dark humor, be aware you might experience some botty tingling throughout the duration of this book. It's not terminal; you will make it to the other side. Trust me; I'm a ~~villain~~ doctor.

That might be a lie.

Still with me?

Then let's get our hero on.

READ ME SECOND AKA THE RULES

Nobody likes rules, least of all me. The day after I was told I wasn't dressed corporately enough, I went to work wearing Converse trainers and leggings. I've stuck with Converse to this day.

Rules were made for breaking.

When it comes to book creation, there are rules and there are **rules**. They're not the same. The issue with a lot of writing craft books is that they're written as if they're tablet and testament: you **must** have such and such a character arc, thou shalt have this plot beat or twist and that shapely archetype.

No.

No, you must not.

Sure, I might throw out some 'must dos' and 'dare ye nots or be slain by the book police' but mostly they're for lyrical effect. You and me bro, we're wading through the same da-fuck-am-I-doing-storyitis.

It's brutal, but it's also liberating. I'm not about to slap hand-cuffs on you and demand you follow every step in this book. Apply what works, leave what doesn't. It's your story.

But there some things you should follow to save yourself from looking like an overly implanted boob: *Grammar*. Aka the technical writing elements - the bricks and mortar of storytelling. You wouldn't build a skyscraper without foundations, and you wouldn't create a sentence without a capital letter and a full stop. That said, even the hardest of grammar rules can be broken if you know what you're doing. I don't. So I leave those decisions up to professional editors and proofers.

But what about the bendy, contortionist type rules? The red herring or extra subplot, or perhaps the removal of a sacred trope. I like to think of those as the skyscraper's interior decoration. Sure, to me, a candy-floss-pink bathroom with matching Barbi-colored bath and shower unit might look like a gaudy nightmare vomited from a six-year-old's daydream. But hey, the six-year-old loves it. And that's the point.

There's a hero for everyone. Don't chase trends. The only person who can write your story is you. If you want to include a cliché, be my guest. If you don't fancy adding tension to that chapter, that's fine too. It's your story. Don't force it to fit this skyscraper. Nobody puts baby in the corner, and I don't suggest you shove your story or hero into one either. A reader will see right through the corporate lip service you're paying story structure, and it won't do your novel any good. Think of the steps in this book as tools and suggestions. Use what works. The rest? Chuck them in the fuck-it bin and move on. You got heroes to craft.

STEP 1 DEFINE THE DEBONAIR

"The word hero is Greek, from a root that means 'to protect and serve'" Christopher Vogler, *The Writer's Journey: Mythic Structure for Writers*, p.29.

What is a Hero?

I mentioned in the introduction that I'd use 'hero' and 'protagonist' interchangeably to save your eyes and stave off monotony. But let's get the terms clear from the outset so you can use the one that fits your story best.

While the majority of novels use the same character for the protagonist as the hero, not all do. Strictly speaking, the difference between the two is as follows:

Protagonists are the subject of the story – it's *who* the book is about.
A 'hero' in the purest form, is someone of extraordinary ability (although not necessarily magic powers) who does good things.

For example, Batman is a non-magical 'classic' hero. He's a normal guy who goes to extraordinary lengths to save the innocent and beat the shit out of the not-so-innocent. He also *happens* to be the protagonist. But your hero doesn't have to be a cape-wearing superhero pin up. He could just as easily be the teenage lout who decides to 'better himself' by saving his neighbor's suicidal dog from jumping in front of a train. Or he could be the drug mogul who sees the light and decides he can't be fulfilled unless he brings the cartel down. Whomever you choose, your hero is the one whose decisions propel the story forward.

On the flip side, the character Hannibal Lecter is most definitely not a hero (what with his cannibalistic tendencies and all). But while Lecter is as far from heroic as you can get, he is an example of a 'non-hero' protagonist. *Silence of The Lambs* is about Hannibal Lecter despite the fact he isn't the hero. That accolade goes to newbie FBI agent Clarice Starling, who is the series' hero.

Yeah, but What *is* a Hero/Protagonist?

The eagle eyed among you will notice that I didn't actually tell you what a hero is; I just defined terms. But heroes and protagonists are more than just flimsy dictionary definitions. Removing the semantic debate between the words *hero* and *protagonist* for a moment, the function of the main character is more than just a plot device.

They (meaning whichever term is most relevant to your story) are the connection between the reader and the author. At a deeper level, they are a reflection of the author *and* the reader. A hero is simultaneously unique and universally relatable. Their traits make them as individual as you or I, but their primal motives (the emotions catapulting them through the story) are the same emotions and instinctive reactions we all feel: love, survival, justice, revenge.

In most (although not all) cases, the protagonist is the one who learns and grows and changes the most. They also take the biggest risks against the darkest evils and, despite those risks, they make the greatest sacrifices.

A Note on Villains and Antagonists

While we're defining differences, I ought to say there's also a difference between a villain and an antagonist. I'll throw both terms around like I'm doing the Macarena. But so you're clear and can apply the right one to your novel:

An antagonist is a character or thing that opposes the protagonist (or hero). An antagonist does not have to be a villain.
A villain is an antagonist because they oppose the hero. But a villain also indicates some level of evil while an antagonist does not.

Of course, there are exceptions. Typically you'll find antagonists in personal memoirs, literary fiction and romance whereas you'll find villains in epic fantasy, crime and thrillers.

Why Heroes Are Important… and It's Not Just Because They're the Main Character

Heroes are important, but not just because they're the main character. They represent so much more than just the 'face' of your novel.

Let's quash the villain love a little deeper and talk about why an entire book all about heroes is so necessary.

Your villain is to your conflict what your hero is to your story. By that, I mean that, your villain IS your **conflict** in the same way your hero IS your **story**.

In its simplest form, story is about change. Think about any novel, film or play you've seen. I guarantee that all of them will start in one place and end in a very different one. And yes, there is always a smart ass who can come up with an example of the 0.01% of books that break that rule. But hush now and let me ignore you.

Your hero (if you get him right) is the character readers fall in love with (even if he's unlikeable). He's the character that hooks your fans onto your storyline and reels them in until they can't help but throw themselves at his feet like screaming angst-ridden fangirling teeny boppers.

Your hero is your story, but there's more...

Gestalt - the Whole Is More than the Sum of Its Parts

In the early 20th century, the Berlin School of Experimental Psychology posited a new philosophy of mind — Gestalt psychology. It was the idea that the mind, in order to make sense of the chaotic overload of sensory information the world provides, created a 'global whole', a kind of holistic reality that is more than the parts it's made up of.

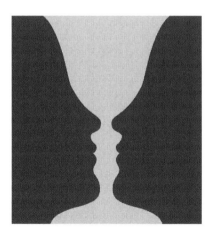

The illusion above is an example of how our brains take the separate shapes and colors and infer a new reality. The candle stick in the center isn't actually there. Our brains just think it is.

Why am I waffling on about psychology and holistic perception? Because that's what your hero is. An embodiment of all the parts that make up your story: change, theme, character, arc, action, resolution and so on. Your readers assimilate those story facets into something more, something real and something tangible. You know that feeling when you finish a long running TV show or book series, and you're bereft? Like someone just died? That's the gestalt of story, and it's what you need your hero to do.

Why Writers Mess up Their Heroes

Writing a book is easy. Writing a *good* book is hard. There's a lot to get right from characters and plot to pacing and tension. I'm not saying that to scare you, just to highlight that — like with anything of quality — it takes more than slapping out some words, chucking in a battle scene and sprinkling a handful of damsel saving over your story to impress a reader.

The most common cockups for a hero are:

1. A lack of objectivity
2. No depth
3. No growth
4. Failure to connect

Let me elaborate:

1. A lack of objectivity

I'm going to make a wild accusation and state that writers are hero-worshippers. Be honest. You've all had moments where you want to shower more unconditional love on your hero than the toddler-shaped fruits of your loins. I know I have.

But loving a character that much usually results in a lack of objectivity in the same way we get blind to our manuscripts. We're all guilty of needing an editor to remind us that the three-page description of the brothel buying market in the middle of your Viking battle is somewhat unnecessary.

It's not that we don't want to see the errors or gross indulgences in our heroes; it's that we can't. We're balls deep in hero worship and wading out to Objectivityland is hard. Nobody *wants* to take the hard road because, well, it's hard! If you're reading this, you know the easy road leads to a case of hero-gout and reader comas. News alert: we're taking the hard road. *Evil cackle*

2. No depth

Writers fall prey to showering positive traits on their hero because he saves the day. How could my dapper knight *flicks blond quiff* in all his polished armor glory *puffs chest* possibly have negative traits?

Because he's human? Okay, maybe not technically human, what with the ink and paper and lack of physical bodily form. But you know what I mean.

The point is you want your reader to *feel* like your hero is human. You want them to feel like they could walk down the local high street and meet them in their coffee shop and catch up like old friends. Which means they need to appear human, and your reader needs to know them like an old friend.

However, humans are not perfect. Not even close. Look at our history of war and famine and genocide. Despite that, deep down, most of us still have some level of meliorism. We want to see the good in others and more than anything humans cling to hope like I cling to caffeine on a Monday morning: hard, frequently and like my life depends on it.

Lack of depth, or one-dimensional heroes are caused by a variety of things including but not limited to:

- **An overwhelmingly positive personality** – Think of being accosted by an excessively high-pitched, annoyingly perky cheerleader at 6:30 am when you're insufficiently caffeinated, unfed and ill-slept. You'll be pretty close to why that kind of hero is a bad idea.
- **Never making a mistake** – Literally nobody likes the guy who's always right. It's annoying, patronizing and makes you feel inadequate.
- **Your hero's personality failing to be a consequence of his history** – Humans are products of their history. Not being a product of your history creates an uneasy feeling, a form of cognitive dissonance like a horror movie when the creaking and high pitched music flares to life and reaches a crescendo... but then... nothing. No bad guy, no twinkling blade or severing of throats. Letdown. It doesn't work. Connect the dots.
- **Not actively driving the plot forward** – If your hero lays down and lets every other character in your story make decisions for him, it's going to make for a rather puny, wimp of a hero. When he comes to make the final blow on the villain, your reader's not going to believe it. Change needs to be earned. You wouldn't expect Neo to go through the entire Matrix movie battling all the agents then let another character defeat Agent Smith.

3. No growth

I've mentioned that story is change. Well, in this context growth is another word for change. In literary terms, your hero is the explanatory mechanism for that change. It's the story of your hero's development and change that readers come for.

Of course, not every story has to have the protagonist experience change directly. You often see a much slower and smaller change arc in a protagonist that has an entire series to develop. And sometimes it's not the protagonist that changes at all — especially if they're an anti-hero (who has a flat change arc). An anti-hero's personality will stay the same, although they do the right thing in the end. You can read more about that in 13 Steps to Evil.

The world or society around your characters could satisfy the need for change instead. For example, if you write a science fiction story, the home planet could be invaded and damaged. Or if you write dystopian fiction, the crumbling of society could represent change. Whatever the source, there needs to be some level of growth and change during your story.

Why?

Because your story hook creates a question, and change is the answer.

Will the hero get over his ego and ask for help so he can defeat the villain? Will the hero be able to overcome his flaw in order to wield the magical sword of villain death in order to save the world? And so on.

This hook is deeply innate for humans, and as a writer you need to capitalize on it. Humans are biologically wired to answer questions.

Who wrote the Harry Potter series?

Unless you live under a rock and have no idea who Harry Potter is, my guess is that your brain just gave you the author's name: J.K. Rowling.

I'm right, aren't I?

There's a reason for that. There's a piece of our brain called the reticular activating system (RAS) that's often likened to being a filter for all the sensory information we're thrown throughout our lifetimes. The RAS is responsible for deciding what we pay attention to and what we don't. But there's a few things that can short circuit the RAS — hearing our name called, a threat of danger and, more often than not, a question. So, when you pose a question to the reader, their brains quite literally have to know the answer.

I like to think of the RAS as your brain's personal beefcake bouncer — you ain't coming in unless you're a VIP. Questions are always VIPs.

A question begets change, which begets reader attention. Change is essential. So are questions.

4. Failure to connect

Lack of connection is split in two:

- A disconnect with the audience
- A disconnect with the other characters and the story

A Disconnect with the Audience

There are many things that make your readers connect (or not) to your story, and your characters in particular, such as how relatable they are, how gripping the plot twists and pace are and whether or not they 'care' about your protagonist.

Of course, creating just the right literary cocktail to connect with your audience and smash the bestseller lists is tantamount to eating a gourmet meal in the dark — half the time your fork misses the plate, let alone reaches your mouth, and the rest of the time your face contorts into a strange set of facial expressions because you're not sure if you just ate Cheerios or octopus tentacles. It's the same for all the literary elements you try to piece together to make the perfect book meal.

Creating the connection between reader and hero is a balancing act of everything I've mentioned, all of which I'll elaborate on in due course. However, the missing piece of the kick-ass hero puzzle is *theme*. And your hero, like he is the manifestation of your story, is also the manifestation of your theme.

Yes, theme is controversial. Not everyone wants their book to be 'saying' something. Not everyone even knows what their stories are saying until they've written them. That's fine. No one's asking you to be philosophical about this. Your theme could start as simple as a single word. Take *The Hunger Games* as an example. Suzanne Collins chose the theme *sacrifice*, and her protagonist, Katniss Everdeen, embodied the theme fully. It's all connected. And when it's connected, your readers connect with it too.

Your theme is linked to the change your hero must go through to beat the villain. The change your hero must go through is linked to a flaw they must overcome to win.

Flaw. Change. Theme. All three are connected, smushed up together in the same sweaty sauna. The reader can see and feel that connection. They need it. They want it. Be a good sport and give it to them.

A Disconnect with the Characters and Story

Disconnect with the audience is an external (to the story) disconnection. The second form of disconnect is more internal; it's with the story and characters within it.

Story

Too often, writers pluck a few traits out of thin air, throw them in the character mixing bowl and hope for the best. We've established that your novel is a web of connectivity which means your protagonist's character arc is an expression of your story arc, which is also an expression of the change your theme denotes. Your character traits should work with your theme and to help facilitate the story and character arc. They shouldn't be an afterthought that forces your dialogue and action to fit the story. Likewise, your other character's traits should fit functionally with the protagonist and with the theme. Married together, each performs a function to advance the story.

Characters

All too often, writers create their hero in isolation. The hero is THE most important character. Of course we should give him our sole focus, right? Wrong. Your novel is a spider's web. Let me explain.

When a protagonist is created in isolation from the other characters and the theme, it leads to an excess of one-dimensionality as well as an eerie disconnect that readers can't quite put their fingers on.

Think about it. When a spider weaves a web, every strand in that web is connected. There might be several hundred individual threads, but they all wind and weave their way toward that central knot in the middle, touching at key points to create web stability. Each thread is dependent on the others to create a complete web.

Your hero (and supporting characters) should do the same. Each character should be a reflection of the others and the theme. By comparing each character to the others, you're able to see how they are similar but also where they differ. Meaning you can distinguish and define the characters with more clarity which produces depth and three dimensions.

And so we come back around to the gestalt principle again — the cast of characters as a whole are more than the sum of their individuality.

Essentially, what you need to remember is this:

While the villain is typically the source of page-gripping tension and turmoil, when the words are read and the dust has settled on your back cover, it's the hero that your readers remember. It's the hero that makes them come back for book two. It's the hero that changes and represents our human nature. The hero is who your readers will relate to most strongly, and who will have that revelation that will give your reader an 'ah-ha' moment. The 'ah-ha' moment is a cocktail of character, theme, flaw and plot.

Your hero is the character that needs to deliver the emotional gut-punch that grips your audience's hearts so hard they have no choice but to read through your entire series. The villain might be the catalyst for a lot of the heart-pounding fear readers feel, but it's the hero they're feeling it for.

Much as it makes me weep, eventually, villains are defeated, heroes are like puppies. They're forever, not just Christmas.

STEP 1 DEFINE THE DEBONAIR SUMMARY

- Protagonists are the subject of the story – it's *who* the book is about.
- A 'hero' in the purest form, is someone of extraordinary ability (although not necessarily magic powers) who does good things.
- An antagonist is a character or thing that opposes the protagonist (or hero). A villain *is* an antagonist because they oppose the hero. But *an antagonist does not have to be a villain.*
- A villain indicates some level of evil while an antagonist does not.
- Your villain is to your conflict what your hero is to your story. Your villain IS your conflict in the same way your hero IS your story.
- Story = change. Growth = change. The hero is the explanatory mechanism for that change. It's the hero's story of development and change that readers want to see in your book.
- The hero is the one who learns and grows and changes the most, the one who takes the biggest risks

against the darkest evils and the one who, despite those risks, sacrifices the most.
- Change in a story is essential. So are questions.
- Your character's flaw is linked to change, which is linked to theme.
- The most common cockups for a protagonist are:

1. A lack of objectivity
2. No depth
3. No growth
4. Failure to connect

- A lack of connection is twofold: disconnect with the audience and a disconnect with the other characters and story.
- Your protagonist's character arc is an expression of your story arc, which is an expression of the change your theme denotes.
- While the villain is the source of page-gripping tension and turmoil, when the words are read and the dust has settled on your back cover, it's the hero that your readers remember.
- Villains are defeated, heroes last forever.

Questions to Think about

1. Think of the heroes in your genre. Can you identify examples of both heroes and protagonists?
2. Can you also identify an example of a protagonist that isn't a hero?

STEP 2 THE WEB OF CONNECTIVITY: CREATING HEROES WITH DEPTH

The Web of Connectivity

If, when you finish reading this book, you've taken one thing from it, I hope it's **the web of connectivity**. I compared a novel to a spider's web in STEP 1, and I intend to follow through with that spidery analogy. Although why on earth I chose a spider when I'm terrified of them I'll never know. But fear not, I've suffered through searching Google Images and all the spidery nasties to find a visual diagram for you.

In a finished book, each part — the characters, theme, twists, arcs, and subplots — are all seamlessly woven together. A published novel has the sexy look of an hourglass figure in a skin-tight dress with no visible panty line. That's what we're aiming for in this chapter.

The Gestalt Spider

In a way, a spider's web is a feat of engineering Gestaltism. Each thread is woven separately but connected to the others. Up close, it looks like a mass of patterned lines and angles. But stand back and you see the full picture: a web, a spidery net, capable of trapping food, something that's more than just the lines of silky string.

This is what your book is.

Your hero is an expression of everything else, the vehicle by which your readers are forced to stand back and admire your story web. Everything is connected.

But How Does It All Connect?

- You have a theme, which poses a **thematic question.**
- Your hero is the positive embodiment of the theme and, through the course of the story, must answer the thematic question. Your villain is the negative expression of your theme and must prevent the hero from answering the question.
- Your hero starts the story **flawed**, on the wrong side of the theme. As a result, she believes a lie and is unable to answer the theme question.
- She faces challenges and **obstacles** throughout the

plot based on the theme (in other words, your plot points, and key events). This forces her to make choices (based on the theme) in order to defeat the obstacles.

- Other characters help or hinder her, each playing a different functional role based on the theme, i.e. providing information, playing the role of moral conscience (or lack thereof), acting as an ally etc.
- These experiences, choices and obstacles shape your hero, eventually causing her to **change**. The change in your hero enables her to see through the lie she believed, which ultimately pushes her back over the right side of the moral/thematic line. Here completeth her character arc! The change means she can find the strength/sword of destiny she needs to defeat the villain. Thus commences an epic **battle** and the villain's inevitable doom.
- Your hero defeats the villain and **answers the thematic/moral question.**

The Web of Story Connectivity

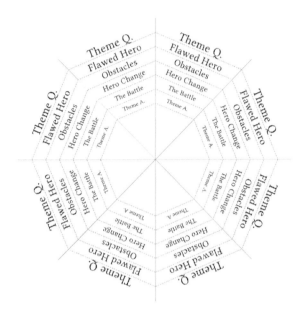

Glorious, isn't it?

The web is used for two reasons:

1. A web is a set of concentric circles. Working from the outside in, you get progressively deeper into the web and the core of the mesh. Like with a story, you work from the greater question at the start, into the depths of the story where it's answered.
2. Every strand in a web is created separately (like story devices) but also connected to each other to form the greater whole: the web.

Everything is connected. Each character, whether minor or major, is an expression of the theme/moral dilemma your hero is faced with. Each character's personality should be carefully woven to portray another version of the choice the hero could make, or as an expression of the theme. Obstacles and plot points should be created to test the hero on the theme/thematic question. In the end, the hero will spiral to one inevitable concluding thematic answer.

Like I said: glorious, isn't it?

Let's take it step by step.

Theme and the Web of Connectivity

What Is Theme?

I need to address something here. I can hear the screams of horror from some writers at the prospect of having to know your theme from the outset. You don't. You can just write. Remember the rules chapter at the start? Yeah, that.

Some people don't know what the theme of their book is until the end. That's okay. No one's going to shoot you for doing things backward or side to side. The important thing is just to write. Often, with practice, story structure becomes intuitively buried into your writing anyway, especially if you don't plot your novels in advance. But it does mean in editing you should check for connectivity throughout your story. Okay, onto theme.

John Truby in *The Anatomy of Story* describes theme perfectly.

"Theme is the author's view of how to act in the world. It is your moral vision. Whenever you present a character using means to reach an end, you are presenting a moral predicament, exploring the question of right action, and making a moral argument about how best to live. Your moral vision is original to you, and expressing it to an audience is one of the main purposes of telling the story." John Truby, *The Anatomy of Story*, p.108.

Your hero IS your theme. **The hero of any story should be the embodiment and expression of your book's theme, and the villain should be the 'anti-theme.'** Let's use the same example for a moment: in *The Hunger Games* by Suzanne Collins, Katniss (the hero) embodies the theme of sacrifice. Throughout the plot, she sacrifices herself for everyone she loves, whereas President Snow (the villain) sacrifices everyone else for *his benefit*.

Pitting your hero and villain on either side of the moral and thematic line creates oodles of vital tension and conflict you need throughout your plot. Even if your hero and villain share the same goal, say in the instance of the Marvel characters Thor and Loki who both want the Asgard crown, the fact they don't share the same morals means they'll inevitably bump handbags and bitch slaps to get what they want.

Thematic Question and the Web of Connectivity

Now, I know in Step 1 I said that you can start your theme with a single word but let's build on that now because having a theme isn't what makes readers flip those pages. It's the question inherent in the theme that creates the need for an answer.

For those who haven't read (or watched) The Hunger Games, here is a short plot summary:

Panem (previously North America) has 12 districts. It controls its citizens by forcing two children from each district to participate in the Hunger Games - an annual TV reality show in which the child-tributes compete to the death until only one tribute remains.

In that plot summary, the single theme word 'sacrifice' could create a multitude of thematic questions. Collins ensures that the thematic question she chose is obvious even in the opening few paragraphs of *The Hunger Games*. Katniss's sister is chosen as a tribute, something that's tantamount to a death sentence. So Katniss jumps in and offers herself as a tribute to protect her sister instead, creating the inherent thematic question in Katniss's sacrificial action:

What would you sacrifice to save those you love most?

This question drives the rest of the plot. The reader needs to know whether Katniss will have to make the ultimate sacrifice and die as a result of trying to protect her sister. The entire series is based on that question. What will Katniss sacrifice to save those she cares about most?

Flawed Hero and the Web of Connectivity

I said earlier that you need to have your hero and villain on opposing sides of the theme, and you do. But don't make the mistake of thinking that the moral line dividing them is set in stone. Your hero doesn't need to be perfect from chapter one. Quite the opposite in fact. While your hero ends up on the right side of the line, usually, she starts on the wrong side. Or at least as a morally 'lesser,' more flawed version of herself.

The reason your hero starts on the wrong side of the moral line is so she can go on the journey your story lays out. A story that will make her change sufficiently so she can defeat the villain. If she was perfect from the start, there would be no need for her to change and no need for her to go on this journey. In fact, there'd be no need for the story at all. But that would make readers around the world weep. So don't do that.

Obstacles and the Web of Connectivity

If we overlay the web of connectivity onto The Hunger Games, then the obstacles Katniss faces and the subsequent moral actions/choices she makes should all be connected. Lucky for us, they are. It's almost as if I picked it on purpose.

Katniss faces several theme/moral dilemmas throughout the story and they're always connected to the theme of sacrifice. Each time she faces one of these dilemmas, she has to make a choice: sacrifice herself or sacrifice another.

Inevitably, Katniss always chooses to sacrifice herself rather than another person. Her moral actions are always on the right side of the thematic line. And never more so than in the opening chapters where she sacrifices herself to prevent her little sister becoming a tribute.

Obstacles should test the hero on the theme. In the example of 'sacrifice', the hero should be made to choose what to sacrifice over and over again. You can weave in the 'anti-theme' by showing the reader how the villain takes the opposing moral action.

Examples of other sacrificial obstacles in The Hunger Games:

1. Facing the opportunity to kill the youngest tribute, Rue (who by rights should be trying to kill her), Katniss chooses to let Rue live. But by refusing to kill Rue, she puts herself at risks. Rue could easily attempt to kill her. But, like Katniss, Rue is on the right side of the moral line and doesn't try to hurt Katniss, giving them the opportunity to team up.

2. Peeta, her district friend, gets seriously injured. Katniss faces the question again — how much is she willing to sacrifice? As usual, she puts herself in danger to go and find the much-needed medicine for him.

3. Collins kills two birds with one stone by weaving the anti-theme in to an obstacle. President Snow uses previously killed and injured tributes and Frankensteins them, bringing them back to life and

turning them into mutated wolves — in other words, creating an obstacle for Katniss to face and using them as sacrifices for a second time.

Hero Change and the Web of Connectivity

The obstacles above test Katniss, make her grow and force her to choose what she's willing to sacrifice. The obstacles push her further than she's gone before. Each time she makes a choice, a piece of her changes. She becomes angrier, more determined, more resolute to take down President Snow's system. She doesn't want anyone to have to make the sacrifices she's having to.

The Battle and the Web of Connectivity

In The Hunger Games, the completion of Katniss's character arc, the final battle and the thematic answer are all rolled into the same scene. The final battle ends after she kills the penultimate tribute, leaving her and Peeta alive. They're on the brink of winning the Hunger Games, but earlier in the story President Snow decided the growing love story between Katniss and Peeta was good for TV ratings. To encourage it, he announces that two tributes can live. But when Katniss and Peeta are the only tributes left, President Snow makes the final blow and changes the rules back: one of them has to die.

The Thematic Answer and the Web of Connectivity

Near the climax of your story, your hero should face a thematic decision. It's the big show-stopping will-she-won't-she moment.

Katniss faces the ultimate choice in the climax — if only one tribute can live, then she has to decide if she can sacrifice someone she loves (Peeta) to save herself, or will she choose to let him kill her instead?

This final hurdle prompts Katniss to have a **thematic revelation.** She's been pushed the entire story to answer the thematic question over and over: How much is she willing to sacrifice for those she loves? She's faced choice after choice and put herself in danger over and over again. **It's changed her.** Made her smarter. She knows they will never beat the Hunger Games the way she wants to (with both her and Peeta surviving), and here is the answer to that thematic question...

Katniss decides the only way to win is to subvert the games entirely. Her answer is to make the ultimate sacrifice: their lives. If both the remaining tributes die, Snow won't have any winners.

The sacrificial suicide pact between her and Peeta ultimately saves them both. President Snow would rather two winners than none. The reason this is such a satisfying ending is because Collins wove a web connecting the sacrifice through every subplot, obstacle and choice, leading you to this satisfying conclusion.

Let's put all this into practice with another example:

Planes - the Disney movie:

Disney movies are some of my favorite examples of story connectivity because they're designed for kiddies. It means the theme, moral action and character traits are usually distilled down to their simplest components, which makes them excellent as examples.

Here's a plot summary of Planes:

Dusty is a small-town plane whose purpose is to dust the local farmer's crops. However, Dusty dreams of a bigger life as a racer. With help from an ex-fighter plane, Dusty qualifies for the biggest race in the world. The film then follows Dusty as he overcomes various obstacles to win the race.

Dusty's Web of Connectivity

The theme of Planes in its simplest form is *courage*. But it's more than that. One of the minor characters, Franz, conveys the theme in dialogue:

"...thanks from all of us that want to do more than what we were just built for." Franz, *Planes.*

Conveying the theme in dialogue is a basic technique. It's tantamount to punching the reader in the face with a theme glove. *Pro tip*: don't punch the reader in the face (it's terrible for sales... unless you're a plastic surgeon). Of course, there are always exceptions to theme in dialogue, children's stories being the most frequent users because it's an easy way to distill a theme into digestible components for younger minds to understand.

Dusty, the hero, wants to be more than he is (theme), which means the moral action he takes must lead him to become more than he is. But how does this link to his traits?

Dusty's positive traits: *courage and determination.*

Dusty's obstacles: *fear of heights, too trusting, Ripslinger - a plane hell-bent on winning*

The only way Dusty can win the race (and become a racer, which is more than he was built for) is to get over his biggest fear and fly higher than any of the other racers. His traits are perfectly set up to enable him to do that. He has the courage to overcome his fear, and when he repeatedly fails to fly high enough in practice races, his determination is what pushes him to keep going.

Ripslinger, the antagonist, refuses to change throughout the story and maintains the anti-theme. He believes you can only be what you were made for. Ripslinger embodies the theme by being inflexible, which means he's also predictable. Dusty uses Ripslinger's habitual race behavior to predict what he will do, resulting in Dusty being able to outmaneuver Ripslinger and win the race.

Dusty's traits combined with the obstacles he faces set him up to test his courage and determination. In passing those obstacles, he proves that he's worthy of being more than he was made for. He proves that you can be more than you're made for if you just have the courage to try. And that, folks, is a web of connectivity.

STEP 2 THE WEB OF CONNECTIVITY - CREATING HEROES WITH DEPTH SUMMARY

- The hero of any story should be the embodiment and expression of your book's theme, and the villain should be the 'anti-theme.'
- Pitting your hero and villain on either side of the moral and thematic line is what creates so much tension and conflict throughout the plot. But remember: your hero shouldn't be on the right side of that line at the beginning of his journey.
- The thematic question should drive the entire plot. It's the question that readers need to have answered, the question that makes them keep turning pages to find out the answer.
- The obstacles your hero faces should give her tests based on the theme. The culmination of those tests changes your hero for the better, putting her on the right side of the moral line and giving her the ability to defeat the villain.
- If in doubt, spider it out. Okay, that was poor. I apologize.

Questions to Think about

1. Take the last book you read and try to map it onto the web of connectivity. Does it fit? Or are there gaps in the web?
2. If you haven't already, take the theme from your WIP and create your thematic question.

STEP 3 PERFECTION PERFECTED

Remember that feeling I mentioned? The one you get at the end of a long book or series — the sensation that something's missing. A hole has formed inside you, and no matter what you do to try and fill it, there are no more words and no more episodes. A bookish era has ended, and until you find your next story addiction, life will never be the same.

Too dramatic?

Tough. It's how I feel.

Countless times an author captures a part of me. I'll look up from the page and wonder why I'm not sat on a spaceship or taking my O.W.L.S in Hogwarts. For days and weeks after I finish the series, I'll long for just one more page, one more bit of those characters because the story was so real, so tangible that the characters felt like friends.

There are a plethora of things that create that effect, but your hero is wedged firmly in the driving seat. In fact, characterization as a whole is the holy grail for establishing the connection between protagonist and reader.

Literature as a Reflection of Ourselves

Characterization is vital because literature is a form of self-reflection. I mean that both literally and figuratively. It's no secret that books help us understand the world. Think of the stories passed down for generations: myths, legends, testaments and laws. Stories were told around campfires while families tore strips of spit-roasted meat off carcasses. Those stories were self-reflective in that they explained what our purpose was, how to live 'best' and the dangers we needed to avoid. These days, our stories are more for leisure than law and protection. But that innate need for self-reflection is still inherent in how readers relate to stories.

Which is why the theme of your book is so vital. Think of theme as the primordial goo your story and your hero evolve from.

The Hero as a Reflection of Us

Humans need to fit. We want to be liked and deemed 'right' by society. We fit by connecting with others. The hero needs to be relatable so we (readers) can conga across the bookish dance floor and connect with him. That connection is what makes us care enough about him to invest in his journey. We want the hero to succeed in the same way we want to succeed ourselves.

Subconsciously we process the book's theme and the hero's moral actions and compare them to our own behaviors and actions. That's one of the reasons readers often have an *ah-ha* moment. When the hero has an emotional, philosophical or moral realization, the reader experiences it too. Why? Because your story is told through the hero, and the reader is connected to your hero. This is some serious Clark Kent shit, people. Whip off the reading glasses, give a little phonebook twirl, and your reader becomes your hero.

Universal truths are one of my favorite parts of a novel; they are the thing I'm often left thinking about long after I finish a book, and I know I'm not alone in that. Realizations leave a mark;

they jangle a person's brain cells into new alignments. I guess you could liken it to your reader's personal character arc.

In summary, what the reader needs to see in the hero is a reflection of themselves. But that doesn't need to be a positive reflection. The most clickbaity attention-grabbing headlines are negative ones. Good relatable, bad relatable, it doesn't matter. Find something the audience connects with and capitalize on it.

Heroes Need to Reflect Humanity, and Humanity Is Imperfect

Okay, we've established the need for your audience to relate to your hero and that self-reflection is key. But how do we create that with our heroes?

Before you panic, this isn't dress-up day at school. You don't need your reader and your hero to look like twins in fluffy onesies. And no one's asking you to find the one characteristic that links the entire of humanity. I've done that for you.

I've heard people argue that math is the universal language. I've heard others say that music or play are the only global languages. But I disagree with all of them. For a writer, there is only one genuinely universal language: **emotion.**

Heroes need to expose our darkest fears, our worst traits and the messy sludge of shit we're terrified of. The easiest way to get your audience to relate to your hero (unless you're a psychopath)[1] is through emotion. Feelings are the most universal thing in the human race. And if you're about to email me to point out some obscure half-human half-gorilla tribal race from a remote part of the Bering Strait who don't have emotions, control yourself pen monkey. I'm speaking for the majority of the population. In other words, your hero needs to be a realistic representation of a human. And the point I'm really getting at is that humans are far from perfect.

We love and hate and rage, so your hero must too.

Peter Perfect's a Prick

Perfection is annoying - cheese grater to the face annoying. Remember the class geek who constantly had their hand up and NEVER got a question wrong? Who, no matter what you did, would beat you by a point, or clip you to the finish line or get an A+ when you only got an A. It's irritating and rage-inducing and, instead of endearing you to their genius, makes you want to fork their eye out over the school desk.

Heroes shouldn't be perfect because it's tiresome and, frankly, it's clichéd. The exception to that are children's books and films, but I'll explain the psychology of that in a moment. More than either of those reasons, though, a hero shouldn't be perfect because perfection is hard to relate to.

Which is why, no matter how much we might hate the idea of creating imperfect heroes, we have to suck it up and rip off the halo. If we're not making tiny mistakes daily, like tripping over words in speech, or the juicy secret we promised not to spill, then what about the catastrophic errors that lead to war? And so, herein lies the paradox for a writer. *We want our heroes to be perfect but, to be perfect, they must be flawed.* Flaws create credibility and, more importantly, believability.

Psychology of Imperfection

The reason children's characters are often 'all good' or 'all bad' is because children are building up their heuristics and understanding of how life works.

A **heuristic** is a psychological rule our brains create. As we roll through daily life, we use the heuristic rules to make judgments on the things we encounter. Having black and white characters for younger children helps them to build basic heuristic rules for right and wrong. It's only as we grow older and have the mental capacity for shades of color that we build our own unique heuristics and develop the understanding for shades of gray (and no, I do not mean the kinky shades. Dirty rotter).

One of my favorite quotes of all time summarizes what I'm trying to say:

> "I think perfection is ugly. Somewhere in the things humans make, I want to see scars, failure, disorder, distortion." Yohji Yamamoto.

What this means is that your protagonist must have a mix of positive and negative traits. No matter how much it pains you to make your shiny girl arrogant or manipulative or stubborn, you have to whip out the negativity bat and beat those shades of gray into your hero.

Choosing Traits

There's no right or wrong when choosing traits. There is an infinite number of combinations you could use, so I'm not going to waste your time telling you the qualities a hero should or shouldn't have. Instead, let's look at the things you should consider when choosing traits.

I'd highly recommend two books by Angela Ackerman and Becca Puglisi: The Positive and Negative Trait Thesauri. They have listings of traits, how those traits impact a character's behavior and ways to show the reader those traits without telling.

Traits Around the Theme

The most crucial factor in choosing traits is to keep your theme in mind. Your protagonist's traits should be connected to the theme and moral action you need her to take.

One of the best examples of a character's traits aligned with the book's theme is Hercule Poirot. As with most detective novels, one of the overriding theme in the series is justice. As the protagonist and leading detective, Poirot embodies that trait/value by serving justice throughout his cases and delivering criminals to the legal system by solving mysteries. However, spoiler alert, in the final book in the series, *Curtain* by Agatha Christie, Poirot faces a moral choice that flips his trait into a negative. He discovers that the character Norton, while not committing murders himself, has learned the art of applying psychological pressure to influence others. So much so, he can influence someone to commit murder. Poirot knows that Norton will never stop, and so he murders him, thereby flipping the theme of justice on its head.

Strengths as Weaknesses

An easy method of giving your hero a weakness is to make them so passionate about their strength that it becomes oppressive or leads them to make bad decisions. For example, loyalty can be positioned as a weakness if it prevents a someone from realizing the person they're loyal to is actually immoral or villainous.

Eddard (Ned) Stark from *Game of Thrones* by George R.R. Martin is an excellent example of conflicting strengths evolving into weaknesses. Ned is Lord of Winterfell, and longtime friend to King Robert Baratheon. Ned's two dominant traits are loyalty and wisdom. When he's asked to return to Westeros and serve as Baratheon's right-hand man, he's conflicted. His wisdom tells him it's a bad idea — serving Baratheon will likely lead to his death — and yet his loyalty forces him to do it anyway.

Values can often be a character's strength. Like Ned's example, a character's positive value can become a weakness. For example, a typical negative embodiment of a value would be justice, and this is often the case for superheroes, anti-heroes and vigilantes. James Bond will subvert the law by doing whatever he can to capture or kill the villain to seek his own form of justice.

Characters as Mirrors

Victor Vale and Eli Ever are characters from V.E. Schwab's *Vicious* novel. Both characters develop superpowers, earning them the title of Extra Ordinarys (EO). Victor has the ability to control pain, Eli has regenerative powers meaning he can't die. Multiple themes run through Vicious, but one of the most prominent is life and death and who deserves to live.

Victor's ability to control pain means he has the ability to kill others (representing death). Eli's regenerative abilities and his inability to die represent life. Yet, the characters are an inverse of each other. Eli decides that anyone with an EO ability is an atrocity and should die (representing death), and sets about killing them. Victor, on the other hand, fights for EOs and to stop Eli, (representing life).

There are other characters in the novel that mirror the theme in other ways, too. For example, Victor, at times, is the embodiment of the book title — vicious. But his number two, Mitch Turner, despite being a giant tattooed giganta-tank, is a total pacifist.

"The two had been in each other's company for a long time. They knew when the other wanted to talk, and when they wanted to think. The only problem was that more often than not, Victor wanted to think, and more often than not, Mitch wanted to talk." *Vicious* by V.E Schwab p.74.

Sydney is another EO in the story aligned with Victor's team. She can bring dead things back to life — yet another twist on the theme of life and death.

The Line Thou Shalt Not Cross

Everyone has a line, the point they can't be pushed over like the lip of the saucepan just as the water boils over. Your hero needs one of those lines.

I like to think of your hero's line as intrinsically linked to his or her values. We all have darkness inside us, we all fuck up and do stupid things, but we also have a line we won't cross, and our values determine the position of that line. That line is one of the key differences between a hero and a villain.

Depending on the structure you're going to use, the hero reaches that line once or twice in a story. The first time is usually right before the point of no return — he's had the call to action and either rejected it or failed to take it immediately. The second time is deeper into the novel. The villain will often attempt to push the hero over the line while trying to defeat him. It's in the hero's darkest moment, the flickers of hesitation and self-doubt that true heroes find their strength. The act of being taken to the line, seeing the darkness on the other side, demonstrates to the hero why he doesn't want to cross it.

The Need for Consistency

Whatever traits you choose, you need to show it (or them) consistently before pushing your hero through his character arc. Consistency breeds believability. After all, we humans aren't creatures of habit for nothing. When you world build in those first few chapters, you also need to build the hero's basic personality, showing his traits consistently enough the reader could predict his behavior, effectively establishing the 'ordinary' world and 'ordinary' hero. You do this so that you create a platform for the change in the hero to occur. It also makes the change in the character arc starker.

Depth from Realism

Writers throw the word 'depth' around like candy at Halloween. But how do you create depth when all you're working with is ink and paper? Realism, that's how. It's the same for a villain. *Stop it Sacha* ***backs away from the villains.***

Sorry. Where was I?

Realism.

Right.

In the previous chapter, I said that a hero must be simultaneously unique and universally relatable. Two seemingly conflicting elements. How can your hero be unique and yet so relatable that his story is universally understood?

You already know the answer: by making your hero as reflective of a real person as possible. Having multi-dimensional traits and a metric-fudgeton of conflict also goes a zillion miles towards helping to create that depth. What separates us from apes (apart from a smidge of DNA and our linguistic abilities) is the complexity of our emotions. We have this wondrous ability to twist ourselves into emotional knots and to simultaneously experience extreme juxtaposed emotions like love and hate, or revenge and mercy, or even fear and bravery. Traits aren't interesting; traits just lay the groundwork for the conflicting emotions your characters will feel. Think of traits as the blank canvas, and the conflicting emotions as the daubs of paint. Mix them together and you get a work of art. Alone, they're no more tools than your keyboard or Scrivener file.

If you want your hero to come across as a fully formed character, you need them to reflect that complexity. Give your hero a cluster of traits and make sure that those traits can evoke conflicting emotions.

Emotion is a golden thread woven through our stories that catches readers at their deepest, most value-driven core. We've all loved and lost, felt the prickle of fear and the sour taste of revenge. Emotions reveal truths and philosophies, evoke memories and feelings but, more than anything, emotion hooks a reader by the danglies and doesn't let go.

The Bravery Trap

It is a myth that the reason a hero is a hero is because they're brave. I mean, sure, jumping off the top of the building, swishing your Superman cape around your back and flying down to save the dame that's plummeting to her death is genuinely brave. You wouldn't catch me jumping out a plane with six parachutes, a safety harness, a stunt bag and a plane on standby, let alone off a building — even with superpowers. But bravery isn't what connects the readers to the hero. Don't get me wrong, I'm not dissing bravery. The world needs bravery. But there's something else far deeper, far more fundamental that cuts to the core of a reader's squishy bits and yanks out the emotion: **sacrifice**.

Think about the videos and stories that go viral on social media. It's always the same. Someone starts out broken, downtrodden and hopeless. Then, after a journey, a battle and multiple sacrifices, things come good and we're all sobbing because the soldier's reunited with his family, or the infertile woman holds her newborn baby.

It's not bravery that's emotive; it's how much the hero is willing to give up that evokes the most significant emotions in readers.

Using the same example as earlier, Victor Vale sacrifices everything to capture Eli and protect his friends. He's willing to (and does) die to save Sydney and Mitch and capture Eli. It just so happens that Sydney's able to bring him back to life again. Handy for a sequel. But that doesn't make the sacrifice any less significant. Especially when there was no guarantee Sydney could bring him back.

When Size Really Matters!

There's an easy trap we writers can fall into if we forget that the size of the sacrifice is more or less directly proportional to how emotive the sacrifice will be to your readers. But the trap is that it isn't the size of the sacrifice that matters: it's the level of *value* that's key. The more value the sacrifice has to the hero, the better the sacrifice is to the reader. For example, if your hero's girl was kidnapped and the ransom was your hero's prize Ferrari, you might think that a big sacrifice. But it isn't if he has three more supercars in his oversized garage. The sacrifice has to be so valuable that losing it for the greater good hurts as bad as simultaneously barefooting it over your kid's Lego and dropping acid in your eye.

In the final Harry Potter book, *Harry Potter and The Deathly Hallows* by J.K. Rowling, Harry has to make an enormous sacrifice. Lord Voldemort is the most powerful wizard the wizarding world has ever seen. And so, Harry, and in fact many other key characters choose to make the ultimate sacrifice — their lives — to save those of their friends and loved ones and future generations of wizards. Two deaths in particular capture the audience's heart: Harry's (obviously: he's the protagonist) and Professor Snape's. Snape is cold, manipulative and selfish. More than that, he has a tumultuous relationship with Harry, and yet he still gives up everything to help him defeat Voldemort. Snape's sacrifice is more unexpected than Harry's and also contrary to his normal behavior, which is why it's the most powerful.

Mama Told Me Not to Lie...

One of the early lessons we learn as children is not to lie. Don't lie to your parents, don't lie to your teacher and don't lie to your friends. But for some reason we forget to teach kids the most important one: don't lie to yourself. So we do. We lie to ourselves.

A lot. Head burying and denial are common traits for everyone at some point in our lives.

But for a protagonist it's even more critical. Lying to herself is key to the success of her character arc. At the start of your novel, she needs to believe a lie so profoundly that it keeps her in the dark about her true ability or power. Likewise, it should prevent her from being able to beat the villain. It's only through her realization that it's a lie that she can fulfill her character arc and defeat the villain.

And, of course, this lie should be connected to the theme.

Why Lie?

Having a lie your protagonist believes is vital because it gives them the opportunity to realize the truth about that lie. The lie should be obvious to your audience. That way, it will drive your readers to root for your hero because they know the truth and want the hero to know it too. Through the character arc, the reader can watch your hero grow and change. But, more than that, readers become part of your character's change.

The lie *is* your hero's dark. The realization pushes her into the light.

When Lies Are Really Assumptions

At this point, while I'm insisting you pull on your liar-liar-pants-on-fire knickers, I should probably mention that a lie doesn't have to be a lie in the purest sense.

It can also be an assumption.

Characters frequently make wild assumptions that lead them into trouble. This is a good thing. The lie your character believes might be as simple as an assumption they made because they only had half the information they needed.

Mirror, Mirror on the Wall, Which Lie Is the Fairest of Them All?

The lie you need your character to believe, like most things I discuss, is dependent on your genre. Tropes are tropes for a reason. For those that don't know what a trope is, it's a reoccurring pattern in fiction, like 'the chosen one' character in a fantasy series, or the handsome billionaire in romance. Tropes lend themselves to character creation as much as plot and theme. The best way to understand the tropes you should adhere to is to read a selection of popular books in your genre. You'll soon spot the patterns.

This lie can be anything from a twist on who the real villain is to a lie another character has told them. One commonly occurring trope around lies can be found in the romance genre. The leading lady will usually believe a lie about the man of her dreams and that keeps her from being with him.

Example: In *Bridget Jones's Diary* by Helen Fielding, Bridget's love interest is Mark Darcy. However, she can't be with him because she believes the lie that another character, Daniel Cleaver, told her – she believes that Mark is a liar and a cheater and Bridget doesn't want to date a cheater.

There's one type of lie that serves as a useful tool for a) deepening your character and b) enriching the character arc. The lie your hero believes about herself.

Your lie needs to be realistic to be believable. And it must be believable to your hero for your readers to believe it too.

Web of Connectivity

That little phrase is back again. Whatever lie you create,

should be connected to your theme. Don't flinch; it's not as complicated as it sounds.

Example: Remember the climactic scene we discussed in *The Hunger Games*? Katniss believes that she must kill (sacrifice) all of the other tributes to survive, including Peeta. She believes this lie right up until the end where the book's theme of sacrifice comes to fruition. By refusing to kill Peeta she realizes she can beat the system by committing suicide, and she closes the loop of connectivity:

Thematic lie *(this is the one Katniss believes)*: Sacrifice everyone else to save herself and win the games

The villain's anti-theme: Sacrifice others for your own good

The theme: Sacrifice

Thematic realization: If you make the ultimate sacrifice you can beat the system and save everyone

I'm coming full circle because on Collins's plot she deepens the web of connectivity by foreshadowing the ending right at the start of the plot.

Katniss refused to let her sister be a tribute. She sacrificed herself and took her sister's place, something that is tantamount to a death sentence. But if you think about it, even in the very first scene, Katniss beat the tribute system before the real Hunger Games even started. Now that is a sexy web of foreshadowed connectivity.

Lies Create Conflict

In the Bridget Jones's Diary example, we saw the lie Bridget believed — that Mark is a liar and a cheater. This lie is special because it drives all the conflict in the book, from misunderstandings between Mark and Bridget to fisticuffs between Mark and Daniel. It fuels the emotional turmoil Bridget is in. If Bridget knew Mark was genuinely the man of her dreams from the beginning, all of the conflict and emotional strife would disappear and they'd be together. Which is why in this story the lie creates the biggest obstacle of them all.

Time the Lie

For maximum impact, the lie needs to be woven into your story from the start. Like Katniss in the Hunger Games, the lie is inherent in the explanation of what the games are in the very first few pages of the story.

Resolving the lie, however, should come much, much later. In a typical three-act story structure, it should be the final piece of the puzzle your hero needs to defeat your villain, which makes it the last plot point around 75-85% of the way through your story.

For example, Rose Hathaway, the protagonist from *Frostbite*, the second Vampire Academy novel by Richelle Mead, has her realization three-quarters of the way through the story.

She spent the first 75% believing that if you love someone, you should be with them no matter what. She's in love with Dimitri. But an amazing opportunity arises for Dimitri's career, an opportunity that would take him away from her forever. She realizes that she's been lying to herself and that if you love someone, you should let them go.

"You can't force love, I realized. It's there or it isn't. If it's not there, you've got to be able to admit it. If it is there, you've got to do whatever it takes to protect the ones you love. The next words that came out of my mouth astonished me, both because they were completely unselfish and because I actually meant them.

"You should take it."

He flinched. "What?"

"Tasha's offer. You should take her up on it. It's a really great chance." Frostbite by Richelle Mead, p.235.

Scars on the Soul

Like everyone, a hero's personality should be a consequence of their personal history. Our history is intricately entwined in our brains, having molded and shaped us until we react instinctively based on those experiences. We've had a lifetime to damage ourselves into a fear of public speaking or a phobia of commitment.

Don't tell me you haven't got one of those awkwardly embarrassing memories that's scarred you for life. We all have. I may (although will refuse to admit this if you ask me in person) have bent over in the middle of an extremely important meeting full of directors and senior people. As my fingertips brushed the carpet and grabbed the pen I'd dropped, I heard a suspicious (and unnecessarily loud) ripping sound. My trousers had split the entire way down my bottom, revealing my underwear. A piece of me died right there in that meeting room and, should you visit, I'm pretty sure you can still find my dignity dried up and fossilizing quietly in the corner. Heroes don't have that same luxury of a lifetime to traumatize themselves — they're spontaneously magicked to life out of the strangely squashy parts of your grey matter. They have no history, no traumas and no scars to shape the way they react or the decisions they make, which is why you need to create them.

I like to call these significant events soul scars. A soul scar is an event or experience that has such a significant impact on your hero's life that it shapes the way he behaves and the decisions he makes.

Tip: It's not just your hero that needs a soul scar. Your villain does, too. You can find out more about that in Step 4 in 13 Steps to Evil. However, there's no point putting a mark in your hero's history unless it's going to be relevant to the story.

Example: Indiana Jones, from the movie *Raiders of The Lost Ark*. When Indiana was thirteen, he fell into a crate of snakes while trying to evade Fedora – someone he'd stolen from. It was from that moment that he developed a fear. This scar is relevant multiple times throughout the films. Like many heroes' scars, it becomes something of a story function and plot point. It's a repeating face-the-snakes-test motif. Indiana has to pass the snake test to prove he's ready to move on to the next part of the story, never more so than the finale of *Raiders of The Lost Ark*.

Know the Motive the Scar Creates

The decisions your character makes in your story will have roots in the scars of their past. Life is about cause and effect, and these scars create the *cause* and the decisions your hero makes in your story are the *effect*. There are other types of scars. Not just fear related ones, but more fundamental scars that can create a hero's motive. In the *Lord of the Rings* by J.R.R. Tolkien, Aragorn's ancestor failed to destroy the ring, leaving a permanent sense of failure and inadequacy in his mindset. This drives him to follow and protect Frodo to ensure the ring gets destroyed once and for all.

Traits are one thing, but soul scars are the inner core of understanding the 'why' behind your hero's motives. If you want to create consistent and believable reactions, that's how you do it. You give your reader the 'why'. No one just flips their lids and goes on a killing spree; there's a long history building up to that horrible moment.

The Difference Between a Hero and a Villain

Okay, there are obviously several differences, but one of the key ones is how they react to their soul scar. I'm a huge believer that there are only two things we can control in life: our thoughts and our actions. Heroes and villains can be twins or siblings, have the same soul scar, and yet react to it in different ways.

> **Example:** Dexter Morgan and his biological brother Brian Moser from the TV series *Dexter*, based on the books by Jeff Lindsay, have the same soul scar. As children, they were trapped in a storage container for days after witnessing their mother's brutal murder. They were surrounded by blood and her body parts, which ultimately led them both to become psychopaths and murderers.
>
> But there's a difference between them. Dexter is adopted, and his new father, a long-term cop, helps him to control his murderous urges by creating a moral code for him to follow. Dexter, having been brought up in a loving environment, chooses to follow the moral code his father gives him and only murders other criminals the Miami police force has been unable to convict.
>
> His brother, however, is a sadistic killer who slices and dices anyone he fancies. Now you might deem Dexter to be as bad as his brother; they are both killers, after all. While I'm not justifying Dexter's actions, he only kills escaped criminals and won't touch women and children. He, at least, has a sense of moral justice and right and wrong. They both have the same scar, and yet one of them retains a set of values and the other doesn't. Although experiences and soul scars shape a person, it's how a person reacts to them that define who they are and what they become.

Everything in life comes down to choice. We choose how we react to situations, we choose whether to procrastinate or pick up the proverbial pen. We can opt to accept our fate, or we can stand and fight back. It's these choices that lead one brother to heroism and the other into villainy. Your hero's reactions to his soul scar experiences define him. What separates a villain from a hero are the decisions and choices he makes.

Nobody ever said being 'good' and 'moral' was easy. Heroes have to work hard for their glistening halos. And we all know that hard work is painful and usually involves a lot of self-sacrifices. Being good is hard. And that's why villains tend to opt for the easy road and heroes the righteous one.

STEP 3 PERFECTION PERFECTED SUMMARY

- Characterization is the most influential factor in creating a deep connection between the protagonist and the reader.
- Characterization is important because literature is a form of self-reflection.
- Humans need to fit. We fit by connecting with others. The hero needs to be relatable so readers connect to him.
- Flaws create credibility and more importantly, believability.
- We want our heroes to be perfect, but to be perfect they must be flawed. And there's a reason why heroes shouldn't be perfect. Perfection is hard to relate to.
- For a writer, there is only one genuinely universal language: emotion.
- A heuristic is a psychological rule our brains create to make judgments on the things we encounter.
- Your hero needs to reflect humanity, which means they can't be perfect. She must have a mix of positive

and negative traits. When choosing traits, try to choose ones that can evoke conflicting emotions.

- We want our heroes to be perfect, but to be perfect they must be flawed.
- The lie is your hero's darkness. Her realization pushes her into the light. Remember, whatever lies you create should be connected to your theme.
- Lies create conflict. Your story needs conflict.
- Your protagonist should lie to herself. It's key to the success of her character arc. At the start of your novel, she needs to believe a lie so profoundly that it keeps her in the dark about her true ability or power. It's only through the realization that she fulfils her character arc and defeats the villain.
- Introduce the lie as early in your story as you can and have your hero realize the lie during your final plot point. It should be the last piece of the character arc puzzle she needs to defeat the villain.
- One type of lie that serves as a useful tool for a) deepening your character and b) enriching the character arc is the lie your hero believes about herself.
- It's not bravery that's emotive; it's how much the hero is willing to give up that evokes the most significant emotions in readers.
- Creating a soul scar is one thing, but then you have to use it. There's no point putting a mark in your hero's history unless it's going to be relevant to the story.
- Although experiences and soul scars shape a person, it's how a person reacts to them that define who they are and what they become.
- Everything comes down to choice. Your hero's reactions to their soul scar experiences define him.

What separates a villain from a hero are the decisions and choices he makes.

Questions to Think about

1. How can you reflect the theme in your hero's traits?
2. What is your hero's soul scar?

STEP 4 THE FUNCTION OF ARCHETYPES

We're all on a journey with our writing, me included. When I came to write this chapter, I naively thought it would be one of the easier sections to write. I'd examine famous books and classic films and pull a cluster of the most-used hero archetypes, their function, their pitfalls, etc. as examples. I should have known it was never going to be that easy.

The Hero Archetype Doesn't Exist

Put your eyebrow back down. I see you all skeptical and disbelieving over that subtitle. But the thing is I don't believe there *are* hero archetypes. Not in the way there are villainous ones. Evil archetypes are ten a penny: dark lords, femme fatales, psychotic serial killers. They slip off the tongue as easy as wine slips down the throat on a Friday night.

But hero archetypes... they're much, much harder to name. Sure, you could tout the maverick cop in a crime series, but wait... that's a trope, not an archetype. Or the chosen one in a fantasy novel. Again — *that, baby*, is a trope. Are you stuttering yet? Yeah. That's about where I was at this point too. Stuck. I felt like a drunk person staring out a rain-slicked window on Halloween. I knew the monster was on the other side; I just couldn't tell if it was Bigfoot or Michael Myers.

So I did what I always do when I get stuck: I started thinking about the purpose of this book, the message I want to leave everyone with — the web of connectivity. That's when I realized I wasn't looking at the hero archetype correctly. Think of them as an illusion. It's not that archetypes don't exist; they do, but not in the way I used to think.

So What Is an Archetype?

Archetypes are masks worn by characters to serve a particular function at a particular time to move the plot forward.

Notice how I didn't say 'worn by the hero'. That's because an archetype is a plot device, a function of fiction. It is not a character embodied in a particular role for all time, defined by their ability to only be that one archetype. Think of it as character cosplay for story pace. If you forced a character to act as a mentor to the hero for the entire plot and only that, you're squeezing your character into such a tiny box you flatten them, literally and figuratively. One of the goals of a wordsmith is to create three-dimensional, rounded characters. That means pouring complexity into a character's design. Forcing your hero or another character to serve one purpose only is simplistic at best and, at worst, traitorous to your novel's potential.

Archetypes as Story Functions

Here's the thing: archetypes do exist, and I will talk about them in a moment, but I want to change the way we're referring to them first.

What archetypes aren't is a type of character. By that I mean I won't be referring to the 'lover' as an archetype, because it's not.

It's a type of character, sure, and even a trope in romance and YA books. But 'lover' doesn't have a function in your story's structure. I've said repeatedly that in your book everything should be a reflection of everything else. The hero is the embodiment of the theme, and your characters are variations of the moral dilemma buried inside the theme. It all gets down and dirty dancing together in a vat of plot juice. Archetypes are no different.

I need you to solemnly swear that from this day forth you'll view archetypes for what they are: a function of the story rather than a hero or character persona. They're a function and not a cardboard cutout character that stays the same for your entire plot. Characters are transient. Sometimes your mentor will also be your motivator or your ally.

Before you charge in, dishing out allies and mentors like candy at Christmas, ask yourself what function you need the character and archetype to serve. We might be parents, but we can still play friend to our children or sometimes serve as mentor and coach rather than always being a dictatorial parent. What do your hero and your story need? Is it time he faced an obstacle? Or perhaps discovered new information? Or maybe someone needs to betray him. Let the story dictate which functional mask your characters should wear at a given time. We all wear different hats in life, and your characters can too.

You might wonder why, if there's no such thing as a hero archetype and this chapter is all about archetypes, I'm still including it. Your hero needs archetypal functions in your story to progress the plot. While I'm sure someone can reel off a list of a dozen books (like *I Am Legend* or the movie *Castaway*) that only have one or two characters, it's rare, especially in mainstream fiction. Mostly, you'll make your life hard if the hero doesn't have other characters to interact with. They provide the parts of the hero that are underdeveloped at the start of the book. Your hero needs the functional archetypes to help him along your story's journey. He might even embody some of those functions himself.

Story as a Person

I want you to start thinking of story as a whole — a real person, if you like. Your hero is the embodiment of your story.

At the start of your plot, your story is a sprawling infant in the blurry dark. Through the plot, your story grows, swelling from events and the characters that populate it and even the obstacles trying to prevent it from reaching old age. As your story reaches maturity, it brings all the subplots of its life together, embodying its life lesson and passing that knowledge to the chosen hero who, in turn, helps him defeat the villain of his story. And so the story passes into old age and the resolution (ending) of its life.

I like this analogy because it's synonymous with the human experience. Readers seek out familiarity in story. The aspects of story that appeal to them (other than the dying need to have the question in the hook answered) are the parts that reflect themselves. The bits of character that make us think, or give us epiphanies because we see a part of ourselves in their actions, or perhaps we don't see ourselves, and that revelation is either reassuring or horrifying in itself.

Story is human because it endures the same path we do. It is born in the hook of chapter one. It grows and develops through the plot until it reaches the climax and, ultimately, its death in the completion of the story.

In *The Writer's Journey Mythic Structure for Writers*, Christopher Vogler goes one step further using the hero in the analogy:

"A hero sometimes proceeds through the story gathering and incorporating the energy and traits of the other characters. She learns from the other characters, fusing them into a complete human being who has picked up something from everyone she has met along the way." Christopher Vogler, *The Writer's Journey Mythic Structure for Writers*, P.25.

Vogler's explanation is oriented to the hero becoming the full person and the characters and obstacles in the plot help to form the complete hero. While I like that analogy, I prefer to think of the story becoming whole because the hero is the embodiment of the story and not the other way around.

The Classic Archetypal Functions

The Friend Function

It's time to whip out the memory jar and dish out the BFF (best friend forever) love. Picturing your oldest bud? The one who held your hair while you ugly vomited in your local nightclub toilets? Good.

Purpose of the function

We humans are sociable creatures. We seek out and crave the comfort of others. While there are a million analogies about islands and lone wolves, everyone knows that wolves live in packs and islands are formed in clusters.

Every hero needs his friends and allies. Just like our flesh and blood friends wear dozens of hats, from forcing our reluctant asses to put pen to paper (motivation), to stopping us from making a mistake (conscience), to being the shoulder to cry on when we've been dumped (companionship), the fictional friend has multiple functions too.

Why it's needed

Friend functions include: motivation, problem solving, companionship, information bringer and (the most important of all) conscience. Quite the overachievers, aren't they? It's this over-achieving status that makes the friend/ally one of the most frequently used devices in a story. If the ally had a recliner in their back pocket, they could double as your hero's counsellor. Their purpose is to help the hero reach the completion of his character arc by talking through his feelings, challenging him when needed and accompanying him on the journey.

As angel-on-the-shoulder conscience, the friend function will ensure the hero remembers his moral purpose by posing challenges when he slips down the slope of doubt or rejects the call to action. When this happens, the friend should force the hero into action, or into behaving more heroically either by challenging the hero or expressing the moral behavior the hero can't because he hasn't completed his character arc.

Friends are like rodents. They're everywhere. But, to use some well-known examples, Samwise is Frodo's loyal journey companion in *Lord of the Rings* by J.R.R. Tolkien. Harry Potter has lots of friends: Hermione Granger, Ron Weasley, Dumbledore (although he also serves the guide/mentor function predominantly), Hagrid and, although serving the sly fox as his primary function, Severus Snape is an ally at times too. Friends don't need to be human. in *Game of Thrones* by George R.R. Martin, Jon Snow has a wolf called Ghost who often fights by his side and protects him.

One of my favorite representations of this function is the unlikely friend. Why? Because there's nothing I like more than not being able to predict a story. And the most interesting characters are the unexpected ones. An ally doesn't have to start as an ally. Sometimes they start as a villain or antagonist before gaining the hero's trust and respect. The Evil Queen, aka Regina in the hit TV show *Once Upon a Time* is an example of a villain turned friend. Regina's character arc is an inverse of the typical villain: it's a redemption arc away from her villainous ways. She gains the trust of Snow White and the Savior and, eventually, becomes a hero.

The Guide Function

Typically, when someone mentions 'mentor' in conjunction with fiction, we picture a wizened old geezer with a wispy beard and a port belly. Think Dumbledore. But let's try to move away from that overused visual, shall we?

Purpose of the function

The guide function serves as a representation of the caring, nurturing and teaching relationship between a parent and a child. Most of us are lucky enough to have multiple guides throughout our lives, whether it be your favorite teacher, the boss in your first job that saw a spark in you or perhaps the successful author friend who took the time out of his busy schedule to help you develop. The guide is an easily recognizable function because it's so relatable to real life.

The primary purpose of the guide in a story is threefold:

Teach the hero, whether that's new skills, new knowledge or otherwise

Protect the hero from the villain's devilish party tricks

Bestow gifts on the hero, from magical death-wielding weapons to the anecdote that helps the hero have an epiphany.

Why it's needed

Well, for obvious reasons: to stop the hero from doing stupid shit. No, really. It is. In the TV series *Gotham*, young Bruce Wayne's guide is his butler, Alfred Pennyworth. Alfred guides him in a multitude of ways from preventing him from selling his family company Wayne Enterprises, to giving him advice on girls and even training him physically for the combat he will face when he becomes Batman.

Guides are seen across fiction, but they do make more

appearances in stories aimed at a younger audience. Younger adults and children naturally need more guidance. And with the advent of the 'orphan' child trope in Young Adult fiction, guides are required more often to provide that parental role.

The Three Functions

I mentioned that the guide has three main functions: teaching, protecting and gifting to the hero.

Function one - teaching the hero

The hero needs teaching because, at the start of the story, he's in the dark, naive and flawed. Naturally, through the course of reaching and subsequently overcoming obstacles, the hero will learn about himself. But guides help speed up the process, teaching the hero the correct way of living, how to use magic (or any other relevant skill) and helping them a significant way through their journey. They also serve a vital role in highlighting parts of the hero's self to him.

In *Dracula* by Bram Stoker, Van Helsing is Johnathan Harker's guide. On the surface, Van Helsing teaches Harker about Dracula's weaknesses, like light and garlic, and that to kill him he must stake him through the heart. This is the shallowest level of teaching. But Van Helsing represents another level of conflict in the novel, which highlights Harker's inner conflict: Harker must let go of the assumption that society is prim and civilized and accept that there are wild inhuman beasts in the world if he wants to defeat Dracula.

Function two - protecting the hero

Protecting the hero is twofold: either the guide pulls a Yoda and teaches the hero about the force and the ways of Kung Fu. Or he throws himself under the metaphorical bus. The latter is symbolic of the hero being ready to move on to the next part of the story. The guide is no longer needed, so instead of just letting the hero waltz off into the haloed sunset, he lemming-style sacrifices himself. *Lord of the Rings'* Gandalf battling the Balrog creature is an example of this, although that particular example is contested. Half the cast of Harry Potter make the same sacrifice, all of them having been in the guide role: Sirus, Dumbledore, Lupin and even Snape. The last example is Obi-Wan Kenobi, who cops it at the end of Star Wars so Luke can escape.

Function three - hero gifts

The last major function a mentor can play is to give the hero a gift. If I were the hero, I'd want a pair of Christian Louboutins or maybe a pair of Valentino Rockstuds, but then I have expensive taste. And sadly, for the hero (and me), we're not Cinderella, which means our mentor won't come bearing a little shoe-shaped box of joy.

The hero is getting a pair of socks or, more likely, the magical sword of destiny his guide happened to have in his back pocket. Functional hero gifts only, please.

Oh, and one more thing. Your guide can't just *give* the hero the gift of villain-defeating awesomeness. Where's the fun in that? Gifts must be earned, Padawan, because realism is essential. Any grown adult knows nothing comes for free. Unless you work in a boys' club, no one gets handed a promotion at work based solely on their friendship with the boss. For most of us rats in the race, promotions have to be ~~slaved after~~ earned by delivering on goals or projects. It is the same for the hero and the guide. The hero must prove his worth before receiving the holy grail. The concept of earning doesn't mean the hero has to achieve something tangible; the act of sacrifice (when the sacrifice is something of value) can mean the hero has earned the right to the gift.

Likewise, committing to a cause, or the act of realizing one's flaws are all examples of how the hero can 'earn' his gift.

Giles from *Buffy The Vampire Slayer* is another example of a guide that serves all three functions. He guides and teaches Buffy, imparting knowledge from his bookwormish tendencies, trains her in combat and always finds that magic spell, long-lost item or piece of ancient text just in the nick of time. Oh, and while he didn't *die* per se, he did get knocked out. A LOT.

The 'Other' Guides

We've brushed up against the goody two shoes of the guide world, but what of the other ones? You know, the ones your mom warned you about. The guide that slides you the pack of fags and give you a lockpick so you can sneak out after hours. Yeah... my kind of guide.

The Negative Guide

The negative guide is one who, instead of encouraging the hero down the right path to heroism, manipulates the hero and leads them into the descent of darkness. But a true hero will only go so far down that path and typically they'll avoid crossing the line into the villainy. However, there's no harm in having a little fun while on the descent. Depending on your genre, your hero might dabble in black magic, forbidden techniques or how to fight and assassinate their enemies.

The most frequent motivation I've seen for the negative guide's actions is their desire for someone to continue their legacy, which tends not to be a good one. They deem the hero (for whatever reason) to be worthy of continuing their legacy. Like positive guides, negative ones are often very patient, although this is usually because they favor pushing the hero through the same hard graft they had to undergo in their youth.

One of my favorite negative guides is Tyler Durden from Fight Club. Tyler appears to The Narrator during a bout of extreme insomnia and depression. Tyler seems innocuous at first. He's a traveling soap salesman who happens to have the same briefcase as The Narrator. Tyler asks The Narrator to hit him and, after some persuasion, he does. They end up in a fist fight which provides some catharsis from the depression. But is the first step down a very slippery slope that leads to kidnapping his own girlfriend and the blowing up of several skyscrapers.

Other examples of negative mentors include the potions textbook in *Harry Potter and the Half-Blood Prince*. Harry innocently thinks the spells are fine until he uses one and it severely injures Draco. Other examples include Littlefinger (Lord Petyr Baelish) in *A Song of Ice and Fire* by George R.R. Martin. John Milton in *The Devil's Advocate*, Alonzo in *Training Day* and Gordon Gekko in *Wall Street*.

The Invisible Guide

While teaching the hero knowledge and skills is most often the primary purpose of the guide, it is not the sole purpose. One function I particularly like in fiction and film is the guide as the conscience. In *Dexter* by Jeff Lindsay, Dexter has an invisible guide: his moral code, bestowed to him by his original guide, his father. Dexter has internalized his guide's code. In the TV show of the same name, we see Dexter 'thinking' and experiencing apparitions of his father embodying his thoughts and helping him with his moral conscience and decisions.

Other examples include Merlin from *King Arthur*, Haymitch from *The Hunger Games*, Gandalf from *Lord of The Rings*, the Fairy Godmother from *Cinderella*, Tyrion Lannister from *Game of Thrones*, Giles from *Buffy the Vampire Slayer* and Sebastian the lobster from *The Little Mermaid*.

The Obstacle Function

Purpose of the function

The primary job of the obstacle archetype is to make sure the hero is worthy to move on to the next part of the story.

Why it's needed

For your hero to change and progress through his development arc, he must be challenged at numerous points in your story. The obstacle archetype is the bringer of these challenges. Their function is to test the hero to establish whether or not he is ready (and by ready I mean has learned enough or changed sufficiently) to pass on to the next part of the story.

These characters are rarely villains, at least not in the early stages of your novel. If your book was a video game, your villain would be the final boss your hero faced. But as with any video game, at the end of each level there is always a test or mini-boss. In your novel, these mini-bosses are your hero's obstacles. In the first and second acts of your story, these challengers will present as your villain's henchmen or other secondary characters. Then, as your story reaches its climax, the final obstacle should always be the biggest, badassist (hush now, it's definitely a word) villain.

As we've already covered, characters often wear multiple function hats. These minor characters and obstacle bringers are no different. Challengers in particular can turn into allies.

Example: M'Baku from the *Black Panther*

M'Baku is the leader of the Jabari tribe in Wakanda. He opposes T'Challa's reign over Wakanda, and when T'Challa is going to be crowned, M'Baku challenges him for the right to the crown. They fight, and T'Challa wins, earning him the right to the crown and the beginnings of M'Baku's respect. When Eric

Killmonger enters Wakanda and threatens their way of life, M'Baku sides with T'Challa, saving his life and bringing his armies to help defend Wakanda, thereby becoming an ally to T'Challa.

Often on the surface level, these obstacle characters will present with a simple physical or mental challenge for your hero to overcome, whether it be a fight, a series of spells to un-magic or a set of questions to answer. However, you can also add a subtext to the test by considering the web of connectivity and using the test the obstacle character poses to represent a moral or thematic weakness in the hero. What better test to create than one that tests the very weakness the hero is trying to overcome? And therein lies the reason why it's a test: the hero must overcome this personal thematic limitation in order to move on.

One of the most frequent methods of beating a challenger's test is to embody the obstacle. Think about crime or thriller movies and how often the hero is captured and then steals a uniform and dresses like the bad guys to escape. In the most recent Ant-man movie, Hank dresses like an FBI agent to escape a cell.

Other examples of challenger characters include the Oracle and Morpheus from the Matrix. The Oracle tests Neo by sowing a seed of doubt about what his true nature is. The test is for him to prove he can overcome the doubt she planted and therefore embody the power he needs to defeat Agent Smith. The Oracle also plays the function of the mentor at different points in the film. Likewise, Morpheus, another character in the same movie, plays challenger at the start of the film. He makes Neo choose the red pill or the blue pill to decide his fate but, like the Oracle, Morpheus plays multiple functions. At times he's also a mentor and an ally.

Fluffy the dog in the first Harry Potter book serves as a challenger. In fact, the entire series of spells woven to protect the philosopher's stone, while not embodied characters, are all representations of the challenger function. They pit Harry, Ron and Hermione against their wits.

The last example is Sir Didymus, the half-fox, half-terrier guard of the bridge in the movie *The Labyrinth*. Sir Didymus fights Sarah and her friends, and it's not until she out-logics him that they can cross the bridge.

Hermes Function

Yes, for those of you who like mythology, this is a nod to the Greek emissary and messenger god.

Purpose of the function

Hermes archetype characters have vital information that they bring to the hero. Often the information they share leads to a change or plot development, the most significant of which is usually the 'call to action' for the hero in the first act of your story.

Why it's needed

Particularly for reluctant heroes, a Hermes character can deliver that final piece of information that nudges your protagonist into action, motivating them sufficiently to take up the call to action. If you look at a range of fiction, guide archetypes often wear the Hermes hat. Likewise, sometimes a villain can be their own Hermes. Heath Ledger's depiction of the Joker is an excellent example of a villain that's his own messenger. Equally, Ned Stark's famous 'winter is coming' phrase is a Hermes-style message.

But, like the other story functions, the message function doesn't have to be a character: the invitation to the ball in *Cinderella* is as much a Hermes function as R2D2 is in *Star Wars*.

Other examples include Effie in *The Hunger Games* and the Oracle in *The Matrix*.

The messages themselves tend to fall into three categories:

- **Good news,** i.e. help is coming; I've found the location of the sword of destiny
- **Bad news,** i.e. winter is coming
- **Prophecies,** i.e. the prophecy Professor Trelawny gives Harry about his destiny with Lord Voldemort

In the original Matrix film, the Oracle is both guide, obstacle and Hermes. She tells Neo that he is not 'The One', which, at the time, is a devastating blow. But it makes him fight harder and, in the end, it's the nudge he needed to realize he *is* The One.

Sly Fox Function

Aside from a villain, the sly fox is one of my favorite archetypes because they're so interesting to write.

Purpose of the function

Their purpose is to feed doubt into the plot and, specifically, into the hero's psyche.

Why it's needed

Doubt raises the tension of the story because it creates questions in the hero's (and reader's) mind. We've already established that humans (in other words, readers) have to have their questions answered, which is why this function is so useful for hooking readers. The result is that the reader has that page-turning impatience and burning need to get to the end of your story. This archetype is one of the most flexible, as almost any character can embody it across any genre.

Sly foxes can come in two forms: positive and negative.

A **positive** sly fox only appears to cast doubt early on but, in the end, they are allies, anti-heroes, lovers or other 'good' characters.

For example, in romance the love interest is usually a sly fox. Whether intentionally or not, the protagonist will (usually as a consequence of personal insecurities) deem her lover's behavior as erratic or fickle and this will cause doubt over his true feelings for her. This ambiguity creates psychological or moral barriers in your protagonist's mind that they need to overcome through your plot.

A **negative** sly fox appears to cast doubt early on but, for good reason, they turn out to have ulterior motives, a dark side and/or are out to attack the hero. For example, Glenn Close plays Alex Forrest in *Fatal Attraction*. She's an example of a negative sly fox, turning from a perfect lover into a sadistic killer.

One of my personal favorite sly foxes is Keyser Soze from *The Usual Suspects*, appearing to be a disabled gentleman throughout the entire film until the end, where his true nature as the perpetrator is revealed. Nikolai Lantsov from Leigh Bardugo's *Grisha* series appears for the first half of *Siege and Storm* (book 2 in the series) as one character, but his true nature as a prince isn't revealed until a crucial point in the book.

Other examples of sly foxes include Scar from *The Lion King*, who makes Simba believe his dad's death was his fault; Dr. Elsa Schneider from *Indiana Jones* and Prince Hans from the Disney movie *Frozen*.

The Joker Function

Purpose of the function

The joker is the character that brings mischief, play and fun to the story. Symbolically, it can represent the need for change within the story. They will usually sprinkle your plot with banter and slap the arrogant characters into shape. If there's a romance plotline, sometimes your hero might be faced with an arrogant love interest, which will result in cat and mouse flirtatious banter, cutting the lover's ego down to size.

Why it's needed

Other than the surface level need to inject humor into your story, it's worth remembering that, even with a joke, there's often something meaningful behind it, and the same can be said of the joker function. Their wit can call attention to hypocrisy, deceptions and dishonesty. Much like an anti-hero, these characters don't change. While an anti-hero has an arc of sorts, these characters serve as the catalyst for change in others by drawing subtle attention and pressure to the wrongness in the hero's world.

Other examples of jokers include Timon and Pumba from *The Lion King*, Loki from both the mythology and the Marvel movies. Dobby the house elf from *Harry Potter*, The Grinch, The Cat in The Hat, Merry and Pippin from *Lord of The Rings*, Odin and Loki from *American Gods* by Neil Gaiman and The Artful Dodger from *Oliver Twist*.

Villain Function

Purpose of the function

I won't belabor the functionality of a villain in this book. Suffice to say, if your villain is weak, so is your story. If you want a detailed understanding of how to master your villain, read *13 Steps to Evil - How to Craft a Superbad Villain*. The purpose of the villain is to drive the need for change. The villain represents the source of conflict and the overarching barrier that the hero must defeat. Note that I say 'barrier'. The villain doesn't need to be a person or being. Quite often you'll find a symbolic embodiment of an antagonist in the form of a personal flaw or a government or society that's represented by a character. For example, The Capitol in *The Hunger Games* is a non-physical entity that controls the districts. The President of The Capitol (Snow) is a physical embodiment of The Capitol.

Why this function is needed

The villain's story purpose is to prevent the hero from achieving his goal. In functional terms, the villain creates conflict and tension, thereby injecting pace into your story and forcing the hero through the plot to defeat him.

One of the major differences between the villain function and the others is that the villain function (in whatever form it takes) is needed consistently throughout the plot. Now, the reason I said in whatever form is because a villain doesn't need to be physical. You could, in theory, write a story without a villain, but only if you retain a significant conflict in your story. If you do, replace 'villain' with 'conflict'.

Let me explain. To fly a jumbo jet, you need two forces: lift and thrust. Without one, your plane can't take off. Without either, all you got is a hunk of rusting metal. It's the same for your story. Without a hero and a slice of conflict, there's no pace or tension to keep readers hooked: it's flatter than week-old roadkill. Let's move on.

I'm going to assume you have a bad guy. The villain should be the primary source of problems for your hero. However strong your hero's motive is for taking down the villain, your villain needs a motive that's just as strong for taking down your hero. Finally, to make your villain rounded, it's essential that you give him one or two positive traits. No one is 'pure evil'. Okay, there are real-life examples of pure evil. But the point I'm trying to make is that we're all the hero of our own story. Just because we're doing something wrong in the eyes of society, doesn't mean we think what we're doing is wrong. Like stealing bread to feed children. What's the bigger evil? Starving children or stealing food to feed them?

The final reason why your villain needs a softer human side is that it makes killing him a harder, more moralistic challenge for your hero. Winning must be difficult on all levels for your hero, and having a villain with heart, or a villain that appears, in part, 'good' makes the act of murder all the harder for your hero. The last point to make about a villain is that your hero should be the one to make the final blow that defeats the villain. It doesn't matter how many allies or groupies your protagonist has, he should be driving the story forward and therefore needs to make that final hit. If he doesn't, it's like you slaving over the thousands of words in your WIP and then letting your spouse write *The End*. Let your hero have his cake. He deserves it.

Crafting the Archetypes - Myers Briggs

Until now, I've avoided giving you archetype-boxes to slot your muscled heroes in. I wanted to push the web of connectivity concept because, well, it's my book and I think it's fascinating. However, I appreciate that while blue sky concepts might be thought-provoking, they're less than helpful for getting down and dirty and crafting the ultimate hero. Welcome, Myers Briggs.

I'm not a qualified Myers Briggs expert, just a mega-fan. That said, I do have a background in Psychology including six years of study, a first-class degree and a Masters. So, before you send me angry letters, note, this chapter has also been checked by a qualified clinical psychologist.

What is Myers Briggs?

The official serious bit...

"The purpose of the Myers-Briggs Type Indicator® (MBTI®) personality inventory is to make the theory of psychological types described by C.G. Jung understandable and useful in people's lives." Myers Briggs Website.

Created by family team Katherine Briggs and Isobel Briggs Myers in the 1940s and 50s, the tool is useful for categorizing particular types of personalities. The reason I find it useful is twofold:

1. It's the most accurate personality typing tool I've seen after six years of studying psychology.
2. The information provided in the personality typing is useful for character development.

The tool has eight preferences grouped into four dichotomies (or continuums). Each person, after testing, will have one preference from each dichotomy, giving them a four-letter code that creates a personality type. One of the tool's benefits is that it shows you how each personality type reacts under stress — something that our heroes will be put under significant amounts of. Likewise, it demonstrates the ways certain types of personality communicate — or not, as the case may be.

It's worth noting at this point, that while you come out with a 'preference' for one or other of the dichotomies after testing, that doesn't mean your behavior is fixed. Humans are complex beasts. We all behave out of character at times, and typing someone using Myers Briggs doesn't preclude them from behaving differently.

Why is this useful for writing? Because at the start of our story we have to establish the hero's 'normal' personality in his ordinary world. That way, when he faces obstacles and problems successfully overcomes them by changing or adapting his behavior, we recognize that changed behavior as part of his character arc. For the reader, change is only satisfying if they can see the work the hero has to do to make it happen.

Myers Briggs can help you identify both how your hero would act in his ordinary world and how he would operate under the pressures of your plot obstacles and his character arc.

The Dichotomies

E-I Dichotomy

(I) **Introversion** - not to be confused with shyness. Someone with the preference of introversion has a preference for focusing inwards. They gather their energy by reflecting on their world, life and thoughts. They often think silently and require time to process information.

(E) **Extroversion** - not to be confused with talkative, loud people. Those with the extraversion preference will focus their energy on the outer world. They will receive energy from interacting with others and a world of activity and often need to bounce ideas rather than think in silence.

S-N Dichotomy

(S) **Sensing** - people with this preference like to take in real information that is tangible. They're observant of the details in the world around them and particularly adept with practicalities.

(N) **Intuition** - people with this preference like to see the big picture, preferring to focus on relationships, connections and patterns.

T-F Dichotomy

(T) **Thinking** - those with the thinking preference are logical and like to remove themselves from situations to evaluate the pros and cons. Often problem solvers, they aim to find a principle or pattern that will apply in similar situations.

(F) **Feeling** - those with the preference for feeling will make decisions by considering what is important to them and the others affected by the decision. They will place themselves in the situation and make decisions based on values and people. Their goal is to create harmony.

J-P Dichotomy

(J)**Judging** - those who like to live in a planned, organized way, seeking to regulate and manage their lives in a structured and logical manner.

(P) **Perceiving** - those with the perceiving preference like flexibility and spontaneity. They aim to experience life rather than control it and are energized by adapting to life's demands.

Myers Briggs in Action

Harry Potter is an ISTP - someone who is tolerant and flexible and often a silent observer who will work hard sifting through facts and logic to find practical solutions.

Hannibal Lecter from *Silence of the Lambs* shares the same personality type as Draco Malfoy: INTJ. They will see patterns in their external surroundings and develop long-range perspectives. They are organized and see goals through to completion. They are skeptical and fiercely independent with extremely high standards of performance for themselves.

For more information, you can visit their website here: www.myersbriggs.org or see the reference section for further reading.

STEP 4 THE FUNCTION OF ARCHETYPES SUMMARY

- Archetypes are masks worn by characters to serve a particular function at a particular time to move the plot forward. In other words, archetypes are a function of the story rather than a hero or character persona.
- Story is human because it endures the same path we do.
- Archetypes are a function of the story rather than a hero or character persona.

The Friend

- The friend serves multiple functions and is, therefore, the reason why it is one of the most frequently seen functions in a story.
- Most frequent uses include: companion, motivator, conscience, problem solver.

The Guide

- The guide is an analogy for the relationship between parent and child.
- The primary purpose of the guide in story is threefold: Teach the hero, protect the hero and bestow gifts on the hero.
- The negative mentor manipulates the hero and leads them toward the dark side.

The Obstacle

- Their function is to test the hero to establish whether or not he is ready (and by ready I mean has learned enough or changed sufficiently) to pass onto the next part of the story.
- What better test to create than one that tests the hero's very weakness he's trying to overcome?

Hermes

- The Hermes function brings vital information to the hero. Often the information they share leads to a change or plot development, the most significant of which is usually the 'call to action' for the hero in the first act of your story.

The messages themselves tend to fall into three categories:

- **Good news,** i.e. help is coming; I've found the location of the sword of destiny
- **Bad news,** i.e. winter is coming
- **Prophecies,** i.e. the prophecy Professor Trelawny gives Harry about his destiny with Lord Voldemort.

The Sly Fox

- Their purpose is to feed doubt into the plot and, specifically, into the hero's psyche.

The Joker

- The joker is the character that brings mischief, play and fun to the story. Symbolically, it can represent the need for change within the story. They will usually sprinkle your plot with banter and slap the arrogant characters into shape. Their wit can call attention to hypocrisy, deceptions and dishonesty.

The villain

- The villain's story purpose is to prevent the hero from achieving his goal. In functional terms, the villain creates conflict and tension, thereby injecting pace into your story and forcing the hero through the plot to defeat him.

Myers Briggs

- The purpose of the Myers-Briggs Type Indicator® (MBTI®) personality inventory is to make the theory of psychological types described by C.G. Jung understandable and useful in people's lives. It helps you type and categorize your characters and, in particular, gives you an understanding of how they will react in certain situations.

Questions to Think about

1. What archetypes do you see most commonly in your genre? Are there any patterns or tropes that appear?
2. What functions do you need in your plot?

STEP 5 CUTTING TO THE CORE

Motive is the bread and butter of character. If you want your readers to understand your character's choices and you want your story to move like a hurricane, then the character driving it — your hero — must be sufficiently motivated to do so. Which means motive is vital to your hero, and the reason why is basic psychology 101.

Humans have a 'why' for everything. Whether it's hunger or emotions driving them to shovel food in or the need to pay bills driving them into the slavery of the rat race every day, *there is always a reason why*. We're rational human beings (for the most part). We take actions for good reasons and we don't make irreparable decisions unless we have to.

'Why' is your motive, and your hero needs bucketloads of it. Without it, readers see through a hero and your plot points seem forced. If there's no reason why your hero needs to go to a certain building where he just happens to find the bomb he needs to defuse to defeat Sir Villainalot, then all your reader is going to do is raise his eyebrow so high he snaps it clean off his brow. There should be no coincidences. Actually, I'll rephrase that: there should be no coincidences that get your protagonist out of trouble. Getting him into it is fine. But without a solid reason why, or journey to proving himself worthy, anything that benefits your hero is a no-no.

Basic Definitions

It's easy to confuse motives and goals. They aren't the same, and your hero needs both.

The goal is *what* a hero wants. The motive is the reason *why* he wants it.

> **Example:** In *The Shawkshank Redemption*, the protagonist is Andy Dufresne. He's wrongly imprisoned for the murder of his wife.
>
> *His goal* - escape from prison
>
> *His motive* - he's innocent and wants to live the free life he's owed

Motive is important because it creates conflict. I said this in *13 Steps to Evil*, but I'm saying it again because it really is that important.

No motive, no conflict. No conflict, no story.

Motive drives conflict. If it weren't for the fact Andy was innocent, he wouldn't be as compelled to escape.

Up the ante, baby!

While a goal can change, a motive is less variable because it's linked so closely to the hero's core values and beliefs. Once a motive is created (after the hero is given the call to action) it's like a parasitic virus. It takes hold of the hero's squidgy innards and doesn't let go until the end of the story. That said, a motive can deepen. And, in a way, it must deepen as your plot develops in order to keep pushing the hero on to the end of the book.

Your hero's motive will deepen during your story's key plot points. They serve as a sort of motive rocket fuel. When a hero is presented with an obstacle, he has to fight to defeat it. Think of a child. When you say no to their request for a cookie, they'll often try and find a way to subvert your decision. Putting barriers in the way of your hero does the same thing: the act of resistance makes the hero question what he wants and whether he's willing to fight for it, which he inevitably is, and so it deepens his resolve to continue.

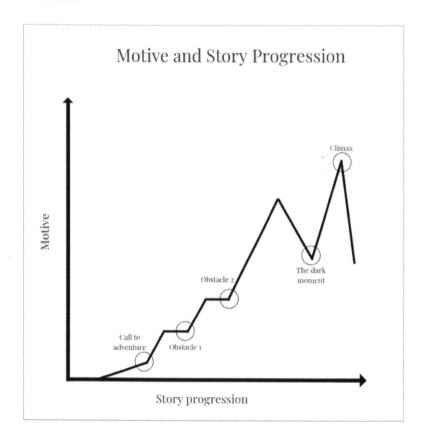

What this shows is that while **a character's core motive is**

unlikely to change, through the course of obstacles and interactions with antagonistic characters, his motivation does *increase* as the plot progresses. Right up until your hero's dark moment.

Motives and dark moments

This concept is synonymous with the famous adage 'it's always darkest just before dawn'. If you use a standard three-act structure for your story, then roughly three-quarters of the way through your story there will be an 'all is lost' dark moment for your hero.

The purpose of the dark moment is to show your reader the hero has lost all hope. In this scene, there should be no obvious solution to the hero's problem. This heightens tension and urges the reader on to find out whether the hero will find the light and make it to the end.

Example: In *Bridget Jones's Diary* by Helen Fielding, we venture through the ups and downs of Bridget and Mark trying and failing to get together. Near the end, they do get together and Bridget invites Mark into her flat. She disappears to get into something less comfy for their evening together. But, while she's changing, Mark reads her diary and the not so nice things she said about him during one of their arguments. Mark disappears, and when Bridget comes out of her bedroom she's distraught. Her motivation to be with him shoots sky high. She's desperate to find and explain away the nonsense she wrote. So much so, she leaves her flat in snowy conditions in just her underwear to run and find Mark. This is Bridget's dark before the dawn moment.

Goals change, motives don't

While we've established that the core motive doesn't change, goals often do. Your protagonist's goal might start as a desire to take his wife for a long-awaited child-free date, but then she's kidnapped, so the goal becomes contacting the police. But when they don't help sufficiently and the kidnapper contacts him, the goal changes to finding her, and so on. Plot points and new information will inevitably push the hero towards new goals, and that's okay.

Surface goals and inner motives

One way to create depth in your hero is to add layers to their character. While that sounds complicated, it's easier than you think. As a species, we're complex because what we say and what we mean are often different, which is compounded by the fact we're able to feel conflicting emotions simultaneously. For now, let's focus on the inner and outer journey.

- The inner journey is what happens to the protagonist emotionally, mentally and spiritually during your story.
- The outer journey revolves around their behavior and the actions they take.

Outer goals

While they don't have to be, goals are often linked to the protagonist's outer journey, for example robbing a bank or saving the princess. Sometimes the symbolism of that goal (and related journey) is slap-you-in-the-face overt, like the physical journey Frodo Baggins takes from the Shire to Mount Doom in *Lord of the Rings*. Other times it's less physical and more task-based, like Michael Scofield in the series *Prison Break*. He's trapped inside a locked-down prison and can't go anywhere. His goal is to break his brother out of jail.

Think of the outer goal as the story goal, which is why external conflict is linked to the story's conflict.

Inner goals

Inner goals are linked to your protagonist's emotional journey. Depending on the genre and type of story, a physical journey or achievement of the outer goal might be sufficient for an engaging story. But creating an inner goal deepens your hero and develops his character arc by giving him an emotional journey.

> "Events without emotion are just flatly narrated facts... Characters without an emotional journey, who do not change and transform throughout the course of the novel, won't earn a reader's sympathy and concern." Jordan Rosenfeld, *Writing The Intimate Character*, pp.48-49.

Your hero won't always be consciously aware of either his inner goal or his inner demon. But that's the beauty of fiction. The reader can be aware of something without the hero knowing. For example, you could show your reader a memory of a teacher shouting at the hero. Maybe the teacher says he'll never amount to anything. Or perhaps another memory of a boss telling him he's not good enough. When your reader comes across a scene where your hero self-sabotages by not going for an audition, they'll infer the cause — he's got low self-esteem because no one ever believed in him.

The inner goal is almost always inextricably linked to the inner demon (sometimes the soul scar). Dusty the plane, from the earlier Disney movie example *Planes,* wants to be more than he was built for (his inner goal). But he can't until he rids himself of his flaw — his fear of heights, derived from his scar, or the anti-theme — thinking you can only be what you were designed to be.

Elaborating on the motive

We've talked about the inner and outer goals, but there's

another way to deepen your hero's motive and personality. **The more detail you add around his motive, the more believable it becomes.**

But that doesn't mean you need to take an exposition dump in the middle of your chapter. Just knowing the source of your hero's motive can often be enough for your subconscious to weave in aspects of backstory without slapping your reader across the chops with it.

Ask yourself:

- Where does her motive come from?
- What wound in her past is the catalyst behind her drive?
- How can you flip the motive to make your protagonist's reaction unexpected?

Example: Eli Ever in the novel *Vicious* by V.E. Schwab. Eli wanted to study Extraordinary (EO) powers — so much so, he was willing to try and kill himself to gain those powers. When Eli successfully gained his power, he sought out other EOs but no longer to study them; he wanted to kill them because he decided they were an abomination.

Connect motive to history

Think back to the soul scars mentioned in STEP 2 — the wound carved out in your hero's past that's led them to the flawed, sensitive mess they're in. This is one of those infinitely sexy web of connectivity moments. It makes sense for your hero's current motive to be derived from his soul scar. The soul scar is a gaping hole, screaming out for your hero to fill it with cotton candy and cherub shavings. If your web is fully connected then:

- The theme will manifest in a question that your hero needs to answer.
- Your hero's flaw will be derived from the theme and its creation will originate in a soul scar.
- Whatever it is your hero wants, he won't be able to achieve his goal until he's healed the wound from the soul scar.
- Thus he overcomes his flaw.

Your hero's inner conflict stems from his goal and the turmoil created when he tries to overcome his flaw and the soul scar from his past. External conflict stems from your story goal, i.e. the plot.

STEP 5 CUTTING TO THE CORE SUMMARY

- Humans have a 'why' for everything. Why is your motive, and your hero needs bucket loads of it.
- There should be no coincidences that get your protagonist out of trouble. Using a coincidence to get him into trouble is fine.
- A character's core motive is unlikely to change, but his motive should *increase* as the plot progresses.
- While we've established that the core motive doesn't change, goals often do.
- There's another way to deepen your hero's motive and personality. The more detail you add around his motive, the more believable it becomes.
- The inner goal is almost always inextricably linked to an inner demon.
- Your hero won't always be consciously aware of either his inner goal or his inner demon. But the reader can be if you show them enough memories and scenes demonstrating how your hero developed his wound.
- Connect motive to your hero's history. Know the cause and the reason for their motive, and show readers how

they reached this point through backstory and memories. Don't use blatant exposition.

Questions to Think about

1. What event or experience from your hero's past is linked to his motive in your story?
2. What plot points or experiences increase his motive?

STEP 6 ARCING ON A JOURNEY

We've talked about how our stories start in one state, usually with your hero in the dark, flawed and unable to reach their goal. Through the plot and the obstacles your hero faces, she changes to achieve her goal, meaning your story ends in a different, more omniscient state. Story is change.

The change your protagonist undergoes is called a character arc.

A character arc is an inner journey a character goes on during your plot. The arc represents the change in your character, where they begin your story as one person and end it as a different version of themselves because of the experiences they have in your novel.

Character arcs are a vast topic, and this is just one chapter. If you want a more detailed analysis of how to create character arcs, I'd recommend K.M. Weiland's *Creating Character Arcs*.

The Arcs

The shape of your protagonist's character arc will be dependent on your story's ending. A character with a bad ending —

such as where they lose something, descend into villainy or don't change at all — will have a different arc compared to a character who manages to overcome their flaw. Character arcs come in three forms: **positive, negative and flat.**

Positive Arc - A positive arc is the most commonly found character arc in both genre fiction and film. The protagonist will start the story in the dark, flawed and unable to defeat the villain. But, through the story, she will encounter obstacles that will change her for the better, enlighten her and give her the strength she needs to defeat her villains. She will end the story in a better place than she started it. A positive arc can take many forms from growth, healing and self-discovery, and usually results in happy story endings. Which is why they are commonly found in romance, Young Adult and children's stories.

Negative Arc - A negative arc is simply the inverse of a positive character arc. The hero will end the novel in a worse position than she started. Instead of experiencing a journey of change and enlightenment, she will experience a sliding descent into villainy or darkness in whatever form that takes. Like the positive arc, the negative one can come in many forms from being corrupted to being disillusioned. While there are always examples of villains with negative arcs, there are fewer heroes with this arc. Michael Corleone from *The Godfather* by Mario Puzo, Dorian from *The Picture of Dorian Gray* by Oscar Wilde and Cersei Lannister from *A Song of Fire and Ice* by George R.R. Martin.

Flat Arc - A flat arc means your protagonist starts your novel more or less fully formed. Your story is less about the change she undergoes and more about the change she invokes in the story or world. Unlike the other arcs where the story acts upon the hero, in this arc the hero doesn't change, and so the novel is more plot driven and driven by the changes the hero creates. This structure is most often seen with anti-heroes or serial stories like crime novels or mysteries — think Sherlock Holmes. Also, Katniss Everdeen from *The Hunger Games* arguably has a flat arc as she doesn't change herself so much as change the dystopian world around her.

No matter the type of arc, one thing's fer-shizzle: you do need a change in your story, even if your character's change is flat and the change happens to your story world.

Start at the End

Most writing advice tells you, when creating your plot, to start at the end. And for good reason. If you know where you want to end up, you can plan a route, create a map and hot foot it to the magical mountain of story greatness.

If it makes sense to start at the end when creating your story structure, then why not when creating your hero, too? Logic with me for a second. If you know what state your hero ends the book in, then you know the type of person she needs to be to defeat the villain. If you know that, then you know she has to start the story in the opposite state. For example, if you know she needs to learn to trust others and build a team around her to win, then she must start alone and arrogant.

The start and end of your book are like north and south for your character arc — they represent polar opposite character states.

Let's work through a real example.

Example: Protagonist Andy Dufresne, from *The Shawshank Redemption* by Stephen King. In this story, Andy finishes the story a free man, which mean he must start trapped and imprisoned. These polar states are often on multiple levels. For example, Andy is trapped physically in prison, but he is also trapped in the psychological torture of being wrongfully convicted as well as the betrayal of his wife. But, by the end of the book, the opposite is true — Andy is psychologically, financially and physically free, but also guilty of committing a crime to get there.

And those two juicy nuggets, dear wordsmiths, give you the bones of a character arc.

You Say TomAto, I Say TomAHto - Arcs and Structure

Character arcs and story structure should reflect each other and follow the same ebbs and flows. Where 'character arcs' are specific just to your protagonist, story structure reflects the wider shape of your novel. Think of story structure as the foundations upon which your character change is built. That means your character change should be embedded within the structure of your novel, which is why we're going to frame this chapter using story structure.

Story Structure - Character Arc's Soul Mate

You'd think that story structure would be *story structure*. One structure in which the myriad of stories could be laid over. But no. Nothing creative is ever simple. There are a crazy number of theories and models proposed for story structure — more structures than bunnies in ol' Hefner's mansion.

But, essentially, they all cover the rise and fall of tension and conflict stories progress on as they edge towards the inevitable climax and resolution. For that reason, I'm going to cover three brief but different examples of structure. But first I want to highlight why I'm talking about story structure alongside character arcs.

The hero is the embodiment of your story. His arc is internal, the story arc is external. The rises and falls of both arcs should move together. Which means you can't talk about one without talking about the other.

"Structure and character are interlocked. The event structure of a story is created out of the choices that characters make under pressure and the actions they choose to take, while characters are the creatures who are revealed and changed by how they choose to act under pressure. If you change one, you change the other. If you change event design, you have also changed character." Robert McKee, *Story*, p. 106.

The three models we'll cover are Christopher Vogler's twelve-point story structure because I think it provides a deeper level of detail than the other two. But, because I favor simplicity, we'll look in more detail at both Dan Well's seven-point plot structure and John Truby's seven stages of story structure. If you want to read more on this topic, check the Further Reading section in the back of this book for more details and recommendations.

Vogler's 12 Story Structure Steps

The ordinary world - Vogler argues that before your hero can undertake her journey of change, you must first establish what she is changing from - i.e. what her ordinary, day-to-day world is. In the first Harry Potter book, we meet Harry living with his aunt and uncle under the stairs. While it's a far cry from where he ends up, it is his 'ordinary world' and one he returns to in the summer (when the academic year — and, therefore, story — is over).

The call to adventure - This is the moment the hero is given a problem or challenge she cannot ignore and knows that she cannot remain in her ordinary world. For example, when a dead body arrives for Kay Scarpetta in Patricia Cornwell's *Scarpetta* crime series, she knows she must take the case and investigate the murder. For your character's arc, this is the first moment your hero is presented with an opportunity to change.

Refusal of the call - This is exactly as it sounds. The hero often expresses doubt, fear or a reluctance to leave her ordinary world and undertake the adventure because subconsciously she knows it will involve risk. If they take on the challenge, they will change beyond recognition and some part of them knows this. Just like when we accept a new job, or teeter on the edge of a parachute jump, or venture into the desert, we know those experiences will change our views and perceptions. A fictional example would be when Luke refuses Obi Wan's request to help Princess Leia and instead returns home to his farmhouse. It's only when he sees it blown up that he knows without doubt he must take the call and join the fight. And so the story begins 'proper'.

Meeting the mentor - The mentor role is symbolic of the relationship between parent and child, or doctor and patient. Here, the hero acknowledges that he must change. Through the mentor, the hero becomes aware of his flaw and starts preparing for the adventure the story will bring. Picture Rocky. *Eye of The Tiger* blaring loudly and a sweaty, boxing, running, stair-climbing montage and you won't be far off what 'meeting the mentor' means.

Crossing the first threshold - The hero accepts the call to adventure and agrees to resolve the challenge or problem posed in the story. As with Luke, this is where your story really begins.

Tests, allies, enemies - To solve the story's most difficult problem (defeating the villain or resolving the major conflict), your hero will encounter either the villain, his underlings or various mini-conflicts throughout your story. To push your hero through her character arc, these tests/battles/obstacles should make her face her flaw — over and over again, like a nightmarish deja-vu. Of course, to keep your story interesting, each obstacle and encounter needs to be different. But the point is your protagonist should face different aspects of their flaw during these tests. In the movie *G.I. Jane*, Jordan O'Neill has a perceived weakness: she's a woman. The soldiers around her, her sergeants and training commanders don't believe she is strong enough or good enough to be a Navy Seal based purely on the fact she has a womb. During the film, she faces repeated tests based on this flaw — strength exercises, discrimination and bullying — each test pushing her closer and closer to proving herself more than worthy, until the defining moment where, 'despite' being a woman, she carries her wounded male sergeant to safety in the middle of a war zone. Thus she earns the respect and position she deserved all along. She also invalidates the perceived 'female gender' flaw.

Approach to the inmost cave - After the journey (and tests), be they symbolic or physical, the protagonist will reach a precipice — the edge of her fear — with success in reaching distance. For your character arc, this moment is cause for pause and reflection on the journey and changes your hero has taken to get here. Your readers will be holding their breath, knowing the hero is about to take a leap of faith into the final battle. Often, there's pause for additional preparation. Think of it as Rocky's final training session.

The ordeal - This is the first of the big battles. It's the first serious confrontation with your hero's fear. In *The Matrix*, Neo meets the Oracle, and he faces the thing he fears most: the possibility that he is *not* The One. The audience is on tenterhooks waiting to see whether or not the hero can defeat the villain. Can they face death and win? The villain will usually strike the first heavy blow, knocking your hero down and into the darkest point of his arc. Here, your hero will falter and briefly lose all hope of success.

Reward (seizing the sword) - Having faced an initial battle, the hero will find, discover or receive the final piece of the jigsaw. King Arthur receives Excalibur, Neo (after dying) receives a kiss from Trinity, making him realize he *is* The One. After a dip in your hero's arc, this is the catalyst that spurs him over the top of the arc. It's the epiphany moment when your hero realizes what his flaw is and how to overcome it.

The road back - The hero must deal with the consequences of facing his fear in the first battle, and the knowledge that she must return to the ordinary world. Often 'the road back' is the final epic cat and mouse chase scene. Your hero's arc is almost complete. They understand how to defeat the villain, they have the puzzle pieces and they can see their flaw clearly. Not only do they see it, they know how to defeat it.

Resurrection - And so the hero must face the final symbolic (or actual) confrontation with death. The villain often tries to get one last shot in. For example, in *Robin Hood: Prince of Thieves*, after Robin defeats the Sheriff of Nottingham, Mortianna the witch stands and runs at both Robin and Marion with a sword. Azeem (Robin's friend) throws a sword through the door, striking her down for good.

Return with the Elixir - The hero returns victorious, having defeated the villain, to the ordinary world. However, he returns changed. His arc is complete, but he returns with something additional, whether that's love, the holy grail or wisdom.

For more on this method of outlining, read *The Writer's Journey Mythic Structure for Writers* by Christopher Vogler.

John Truby's Seven Stages of Story Structure

Weakness and need

At the start of your novel, your hero should not be aware of his weakness. Why? Because the flaw is inextricably linked to his character arc. The character arc is the journey your hero takes to overcome his weakness. The villain is usually a symbol or manifestation of the opposite state of the hero's flaw, which is why defeating the villain enables the hero to overcome his inherent flaw/need.

Desire

This is what the hero wants — the goal of the story. But desire and need are different. Need is internal to the hero, desire is external and connected to the story. Think of them as inner and outer goals, like in Step 5.

"Need has to do with overcoming a weakness within the character. A hero with a need is aways paralyzed in some way at the beginning of the story by his weakness." John Truby, *The Anatomy of Story*, p.44.

In essence, need is what creates the change in the hero (the hero needs to overcome his flaw), but the desire is based in the external story. The story is where the hero's need is placed so the reader has an expression of the hero's need. Needs and desires must be relevant to the protagonist and the story. No one cares if John Smith wants to save enough money to plant a plum/prune farm to help his mother's irritable bowels. But the audience will care if, in order to get the money, John has to rob a bank and kill the banker.

Opponent

We all know we need a bad guy. Truby simply says you should pick the best character to be the villain. Sounds obvious, but he means you should pick the character who:

1. can strike the hero in the precious parts and attack his weakness most effectively, and
2. the character who wants (at the deepest level) the same thing as the hero, as this produces the most significant conflict.

Plan

This is the plan the protagonist creates to reach his goal. It's the vertebrae making up your story's spine. It will include the key events leading the reader from the first page to the final climax, and inherent in the plan are all the obstacles the hero must face to defeat their flaw.

Battle

This is the battle in which you pit hero against villain (or hero against flaw). The tension should continue to rise through your story as a result of repeated interactions between your hero and villain. During the earlier interactions, the hero will lose to the villain because he is still flawed. The villain knows the hero is flawed and is able to utilize his flaw against him. But as the confrontations reach the climax of your novel, the hero will have a self-revelation allowing him to understand how he must change to defeat the villain and overcome his flaw. Thus commences the final battle, in which the hero finally defeats the villain.

Self-Revelation

A point to note: unless you're extremely careful, having your protagonist state their revelation will make your story sound preachy. There's no need for the exposition. Your hero should be able to demonstrate the revelation he's had through his actions. This is the tipping point of the character arc — the moment in which he reaches the highest peak — the revelation, the defeat of the flaw — and then tips over to race back to what Truby calls the new equilibrium (or, as Vogler would say, the ordinary world).

New equilibrium

The villain has been defeated, the hero's flaw is vanquished and life can return to its new normal. New because a part of the hero will be changed permanently. Whether that be for the positive or negative depends on her character arc.

Dan Wells's Seven-Point Plot Plan

The last type of structure is from Dan Wells. He gives a fantastic set of lectures on story structure and the seven-point plot plan. You can see the full lecture series on YouTube here: https://www.youtube.com/playlist?list=PLC430F6A783A88697 The reason I've included his story structure model is twofold. First, it's the simplest of the three models. Second, Wells makes a suggestion as to the order in which you should create your story structure. So, not only does Wells give you a framework on which to work, but he also gives you a torch and a freaking map to boot.

The elements of Wells's plot structure, in the **chronological order** of your story, are as follows:

- Hook
- Plot turn 1
- Pinch 1
- Midpoint
- Pinch 2
- Plot turn 2
- Resolution

The below is an explanation of the elements in the order in which Wells suggests you tackle them:

1. **Resolution.** Wells (along with Truby, along with me) argues that you should start with the ending. Why? Because if you're going for a walk, you need to know where you're going to decide which direction to travel. If you have an endpoint, you can create a map. Everything in your story will lead to this point. As I've already mentioned, if you know how your character's arc ends

you know who she needs to be at the start and the journey she needs to go on.

2. **Hook** is the next element Wells suggests you work on. The hook is the opposite of the resolution. In other words, the beginning. What is the opposite state to the ending? That's where your character arc begins. In technical terms, the 'hook' is the literary device you use in the first few pages of your story to reel your readers into the rest of the novel. Often, it's a question implied in your opening — a question your readers can only get the answered by devouring the rest of your book. For example, an unexplained dead body that shows up.

3. The **Midpoint** is the third element you should focus on. The midpoint is the moment in the story where your protagonist moves from reaction to action. In a character arc, it's the point where the hero takes charge and no longer wants to 'be done to'. The term 'midpoint' is used loosely as it doesn't need to be the physical middle of your book but the 'middle' of the story indicated by the change in behavior from the hero — no longer passive, but actively driving the story.

4. **Plot Turn 1** is the fourth element you should focus on. This is where you introduce the first real moments of conflict or twist. This is where your hero starts her tests, faces the reality of her flaw and realizes she needs to be better to win. Your villain should be introduced at this point (if they haven't been already). This plot turn is where your villain applies enough pressure on the hero that it pushes the hero from the hook to the midpoint.

5. **Plot Turn 2** is where you focus next. This plot turn moves you from your story's midpoint towards the ending. It's the moment in the story where your protagonist obtains the final piece of the puzzle (or weapon, or has the self-revelation) needed to defeat the villain. For example, in the Matrix movie, this is the moment Neo realizes he is The One.

6. **Pinch 1** this is the sixth element. Pressure should be applied to your hero, i.e. an obstacle or barrier or interaction with the

villain or an underling. It should also force the characters into action.

7. **Pinch point 2** - You work on this last. Apply even more pressure. Make the situation seem hopeless for the hero. Remember the 'dark moment'? That.

Connect It, Baby

I'll pause here for a second and bring it back my love child, the web of connectivity. Plot and theme connect seamlessly. No matter what you call them, most stories have the following key elements:

- **A plot point,** where something significant happens.
- **A pinch point,** where the villain ramps up the pressure.
- **Turning points,** usually a significant event in favor of the hero.

At each of these points, you need to bury the theme into your story, whether it be through character action, decision, dialogue or a theme-based obstacle. Grab the theme (and a shovel), dig a hole in your book and bury it.

You need to do a Hansel and Gretel and drop theme-shaped breadcrumbs within your story's plot points, scenes and characters' actions. Every crumb you lay down is another clue for your readers to pick up and follow until they find your glorious thematic conclusion.

These breadcrumbs are clever little bastards. They make the reader go on the journey with your hero. It makes them feel like they have the thematic revelation *personally*. Instead of the hero explaining his epiphany, the reader has the 'ah ha' moment with them. And that nifty little trickster is how you connect that web and leave your reader with your book's essence. It's the ultimate

book hangover full of magic and bookish ghosts that will haunt
them for eternity.

The Principles of Story Arcs

Although brief, we've covered three different methods for
structuring your story (and therefore character) arc. Each story
will create a different variation of story structure, but that's to be
expected. The principles though will always stay the same, but
I'll talk about that in a second. I started this book by telling you
rules are made to be broken, and that's precisely why I showed
you three different structure models for story.

If your hero has a negative arc, your story will naturally be an
inversion of a positive arc. If you have a more social or philosophical point to make, then maybe a flat arc is right for you. Whatever your story, be bold, be fierce, break the rules and experiment
with structure.

Mirror, Mirror on the Wall, Which Is the Simplest Arc of Them All?

I don't want to repeat the arc and structure stuff I've just gone
through, but it's worth noting the commonalities between them
all. Which, in my typical style, has been paired down to the abso-
lute simplest form:

Flawed hero - *All stories start with an inadequate hero. That is
the purpose of the story: to push him through enough experiences he
will become a better person.*

Hero has goal - *The hero's goal and desire is what ultimately
pulls him into the story and makes him take the call to action.*

Hero tries to achieve goal and fails repeatedly - *These are the
obstacles and challenges your hero faces during the plot.*

Hero has a realization – *The hero discovers why he's failing and* *gains a magical item or newfound strength or insight that enables him to succeed.*

Hero achieves goal – *The villain's defeated, the hero's flaw is banished, the party's started... wait... ignore that last bit.*

Back to normal life - *The story is complete and life returns to the new normal.*

And now to some principles.

Double up on the Weak Front

Giving your hero a moral weakness as well as a psychological weakness deepens the complexity and believability of your protagonist. It also gives him another thing to overcome in his character arc.

Moral weaknesses are derived from psychological weaknesses. Whatever the psychological weakness is, an immoral behavior can extend from it.

Example: Cady Heron from the movie *Mean Girls* is weak because she's agreeable. So agreeable she refuses to create any conflict even when it's needed. This results in her joining a popular group of girls at school. Despite having a secret plan to take these popular girls down, her agreeable nature leads to a moral flaw. She ends up hurting her real friends in her plight to defeat the popular girls.

Good Plot Problems, Bad Plot Problems

You need to create a plot problem good enough that your hero can't refuse the challenge. Of course, sometimes change is forced upon your hero (rules are always made for breaking, after all). But the problem should create a pull on the hero's emotions and values. So much so, he has no choice but to take the journey through your story. Make the journey mean something.

Lies and Choices

We've already discussed the lie your hero believes in Step 3 but, after his self-realization, the hero is often posed with a question. It might be an implied question rather than through dialogue:

Should the hero open Pandora's box? Should Ned Stark choose justice or loyalty? It has to be a choice your hero can't wriggle out of.

Whatever the choice, it should be difficult to make, which means it can't be as simple as 'kill the villain to save the dame' or 'don't kill the bad guy and let the dame die'. That's not a choice: there is no choice there. The answer is far too obvious and any hero worth their salt would choose to slay the villain in a demonstration of muscled torso and oil-slicked biceptery.

So, then, what actually makes a difficult choice a difficult choice? What pits a lame choice apart from a juicy one? Well, juicy choices make the hero wriggle and writhe under the weight of it. A choice is only tricky if the options you have to choose from are similar or have similar outcomes. Offering someone licorice and vomit flavored ice cream or a scoop of strawberry isn't a choice. But, between strawberry and raspberry, it might be. Likewise, pitting two moral values against each other creates inner conflict — like Ned Stark's experience of trying to choose between his loyalty and his wisdom.

It works the same way if you pit the decision negatively between two evils. For example, in *Sophie's Choice* written by William Styron, the protagonist, Sophie, is made to choose which of her two children must die by gassing during the Holocaust. Neither outcome is positive, and ultimately the choice she makes leads her down a dark path she can never recover from.

Change, like Rewards, Must Be Earned

See, *this* is the difference between us chunky monkey humans and your flat on the page characters. We breathers get the benefit of the doubt. Your characters do not. Any change they undergo must be fought for and earned.

Your hero has an entire novel to try and get what she wants. Why would you give it to her after her first mini battle? That's like getting down and dirty on a first date. Unless you're a total hero slut, don't do the dirty. Don't give her what she wants in the first act. Treat them mean to keep them keen. Make your hero work for it, throw in some Rocky training montages, a quest or five and a few fisticuffs. It's far more interesting for the reader.

Essentially, you need to torture your hero before giving her what she wants. Now, try not to roll out the battle cannons and profess that you could never torture your darling, because *tough*. You gotta whip out the flail and wooden stocks and flip the switch on your empathy. The only thing you should be getting down and dirty with is some full-blown hero torment.

Why do you need to torture your hero?

Because of believability.

Everyone knows that getting what you want in life (and fiction) is hard. The universe actively tests you and puts barriers and obstacles in your way. Some days you'll take ten steps forward, other days you'll be knocked back and feel broken and lost. Even the most successful people in the world have experienced failures and setbacks. It's a kind of universal torture!

"When I got a rejection slip from AHMM, I pounded a nail into the wall above the Webcor, wrote 'Happy Stamps' on the rejection slip, and poked it onto the nail... By the time I was fourteen... the nail in my wall would no longer support the weight of the rejection slips impaled upon it." Stephen King, *On Writing*, pp.33-34.

Some of the most famous real heroes and leaders have found the path to success impossibly hard. For example:

- 5127 - the number of failed prototypes James Dyson made before finally creating the first bagless vacuum cleaner.
- 2 - the number of times Steven Spielberg was rejected by the University of Southern California's School of Cinematic Arts.
- 4 - the age Albert Einstein was before he could speak.
- J.K. Rowling was broke, depressed and about to be bankrupt before she sold Harry Potter.

While I was being semi-facetious about torturing your protagonist, whatever their goal is, it needs to be exceptionally hard to achieve. But, more importantly, the journey to their goal should be emotional and heart-wrenching, because people change when they're pushed to their limits.

Your protagonist needs to suffer and make sacrifices if they want to win. But remember: as much as your hero wants to win, so does your villain. Do you think General Zod will just roll over and let Superman save Metropolis? Don't think so. You wouldn't find Usain Bolt slowing down in the 100m sprint no matter how many times he won.

The challenge must be so acute that part of your hero has to change fundamentally to win. John Truby, in *The Anatomy of a Story*, goes as far as saying:

"In a good story, as the hero goes after a goal, he is forced to challenge his most deep-seated beliefs. In the cauldron of crisis, he sees what he really believes, decides what he will act on, and then takes moral action to prove it." p.80.

Do you know the next line Stephen King wrote after the nail fell down from the weight of rejection slips?

"I replaced the nail with a spike and went on writing." Stephen King, *On Writing*, p.34.

That's exactly what your hero should do – pull up his big girl pants and carry on fighting.

Dexter Morgan, created by Jeff Lindsay and famous both for the *Dexter* books and TV series, is one of my favorite examples of a tortured protagonist.

Plot Summary: Dexter Morgan is a blood spatter analyst for the Miami police department, he also moonlights as a serial killer. The twist is that he only kills bad guys that meet a specific code: he has to be sure of their guilt, and the police have to have failed to capture them. The series follows Dexter as he commits these murders and the spiraling problems being a serial killer *and* trying to lead a family life creates.

Lindsay tortures Dexter in three key ways:

Mental Torture:

Dexter works for the police force, the very people who would jail him for the murders he commits. This means he has to hide who he is and all the psychotic shenanigans he gets up to twenty-four hours a day. In one season, another killer, the Ice Truck Killer, comes on the scene and threatens to expose Dexter's secret life. Dexter discovers that the Ice Truck Killer is actually his real brother, who he was separated from as a child. Dexter's brother (the Ice Truck Killer) also then dates Dexter's adopted sister as a kind of twisted torture, putting Dexter under intense pressure while trying to juggle his secret life, his family, protecting his sister and his blood spatter analyst job. It leaves him exhausted, exposed, vulnerable and, quite frankly, the audience (and me) on the edges of our seats.

Physical Torture:

Granted, sprinkling a spot of military stress torture and fingernail removing might not be appropriate for children's fiction. However, depending on your genre, physical torture might well be an option, even if you don't think it is. For example, even if you're writing a chick lit book, you can physically torture your character. Make them take a long, arduous, physically demanding journey to their lover. And why not chuck in a few obstacles along the way?

During the show, Dexter was beaten and tortured on a number of occasions. Despite his serial killing habit, the audience still sympathizes with him when he's tortured or captured because — 'killer actions' aside — Dexter has several traits of a hero. He has a moral line he won't cross (his code), he tries to do the right thing, he protects his family, and deep down most of us relate to vigilante justice.

Moral Torture:

Moral torture has always been one of my favorite forms of character pain. There's something fundamentally brutal about making a (character) have to choose between the things he values most. It plays on reader fears: what will the hero do? What would they do? Will the hero choose loyalty or justice? Moral torture creates a natural 'moral' question: will the hero stick to her morals or will she cross the line to get the justice she desires? It comes back to human psychology and the need to have our questions answered. This keeps the reader on the edge of their seat.

Dexter has managed to evade police capture by adhering strictly to 'the code' which his dad helped him develop. Dexter only kills criminals if they meet the code. But, throughout the series, we watch as innocent people who don't match the code start to get suspicious of his behavior and even threaten to expose him. This tests his moral fiber and everything he believes in: if he goes against his code then he's the same as the common murderers he's trying to get rid of. It's his moral code that makes him interesting and what drives the viewer to keep watching to find out what he will do, and how far he can be pushed before he will break his code.

Dexter's character arc is a fascinating one because he's an anti-hero. Anti-heroes, by their nature, don't change. They make better decisions, and ultimately do the right thing, but they retain whatever negative personality traits they had at the start. Their character arcs are effectively flat. At the end of the series, Dexter cannot give up his serial killing ways. But the realization he comes to is that unless he gives up his son and girlfriend, he will continue to endanger them. His sacrifice is his character change. Instead of killing his way to what he wants, he lets go of the only things he cares about (his family) and leaves them to be free.

Thoughts on Series Arcs

Writing a series is a wise marketing choice. You can use your first book as a loss leader to generate a huge volume of sales to get readers to read through the other books in your series (which is where you make your pennies). But writing a series poses three issues for your protagonist:

- Readers come to a series for continuity, which creates problem two:
- How do you create character continuity when you need to generate character arcs in each book?
- You need a series arc too.

Readers come to a series for continuity because they like the familiar comfort of well-worn characters. It's like a child's comfort blanket or your favorite shirt. Genre and character tropes mean your readers know what's coming and they love it anyway. It's what causes readers to stick to one or two favorite genres when choosing their next book.

A series arc is, simply, the arc your story follows across every book in your series. If your book was the ocean, your series arc would be the undercurrent and each book arc would be made up of surface waves. What often happens is that the hero will face a different villain in each book, or the same villain but with a different method of attack in each book. Overarching all of the individual book duels will be a bigger problem, whether it's a bigger 'grand' villain, or perhaps the gradual decline of a society (often in dystopian series like *The Hunger Games* or *Divergent*).

Here's an example:

Harry Potter faces a variety of villains throughout the books, from Dark Arts teachers to Dementors and Draco Malfoy, but bubbling under the skin of all of them is his long-running battle against arch nemesis Lord Voldemort. Voldemort is ever present in each book, albeit less so in the earlier books. As Harry defeats the minor villains in each successive book, Voldemort becomes more and more significant until Harry and Voldemort reach their epic final battle in the conclusion of the series.

There are various series arcs you can use but the three most often seen are as follows:

Groundhog Day Arc – The hero in this series *never* changes, no matter how many books there are in your series. Often the protagonist will be an anti-hero rather than a pure hero. Examples include series and characters like James Bond or Sherlock Holmes. Interestingly, individual story arcs are often the same too. In crime books a body is found, the detective works the case, unearths clues and discovers the killer.

Slow Burn Arc – Some protagonists mature over the entire series. They repeat mistakes and often encounter similar obstacles (albeit in different forms) throughout the series. They have one or two major flaws they need to overcome, but they don't achieve this until the end of the series. Examples include Harry Potter, who works on leadership and confidence and the realization that he needs to make the same sacrifice his mother did for those he loves: his life. He isn't strong enough to defeat Voldemort until the final book.

Multiple Stories, Multiple Problems – The last type of series arc occurs when the protagonist faces a new problem or flaw in each book. Each new story results in him having to overcome a new flaw or problem. This is the hardest type of arc to use in a series because having a new flaw or problem each time means there's less opportunity for continuity. However, it also makes for excellent lessons-learned type stories which are more often found in children's fiction. For example, Woody from *Toy Story* has to overcome his jealousy of Buzz Lightyear in the first film, move past his ego in favor of his heart in the second movie and, in the final film, he has to let go of the past.

STEP 6 ARCING ON A JOURNEY SUMMARY

- A character arc is an inner journey a character goes on during your plot. The arc represents the change in your character, where they begin your story as one person and end it having grown and developed into a different version of themselves as a result of the experiences in your novel.
- Character arcs come in three forms: **positive, negative and flat.**
- Story is change.
- The start and end of your book are like north and south for your character arc. They represent polar opposite character states. Start at the end so you can create a map to guide you through to the end.
- The challenge in your story must be so acute that part of your hero has to change irrevocably to win.
- Think of story structure as the foundations upon which your character change is built.
- Try to bury the theme within your story's plot points, scenes and characters' actions.

- **Flawed hero** - *all stories start with an inadequate hero — that is the purpose of the story — to push him through enough experiences he will become a better person.*
- **The hero has goal** - *the hero's goal and desire is what ultimately pulls him into the story, and makes him take the call to action.*
- **The hero tries to achieve goal and fails repeatedly** - *these are the obstacles and challenges your hero faces during the plot.*
- **The hero has a realization** – *the hero discovers why he's failing and gains a magical item or newfound strength or insight that enables him to succeed.*
- **The hero achieves goal** – *the villain's defeated, the hero's flaw is banished.*
- **Back to normal life** - *the story is complete and life returns to the new normal.*

- Torture your hero. That is all.

Series Arcs

- **Groundhog Day arc** – the hero in this series *never* changes no matter how many books there are in your series.
- **Slow Burn arc** – some protagonists mature over the entire series. They repeat mistakes and often encounter similar obstacles (albeit in different forms) throughout the series.
- **Multiple Stories, Multiple Problems** – the last type of series arc is where the protagonist faces a new problem or flaw in each book.

Questions to Think about

1. What type of series arc do you have?
2. What type of character arc does your hero have?

STEP 7 CRAFTING CONFLICT

I often hear writers weeping over the complexity of creating conflict. But, in reality, when you break 'conflict' down to its itty-bitty components, it's as simple as:

A + B = C

Or

The existence of a goal + prevention of the goal being achieved = conflict.

That's it.

Okay, I'm being a smidge facetious because, of course, there are a bunch of ways you can create conflict. But those ways almost always plastic wrap an author into a subplot hell-mare. Still. The point is, if you wipe away the subplots, dust down the descriptive prose and banish the witty dialogue, you can get to the core of conflict:

Create a goal... Stop the goal coming to fruition.

There are two questions you should keep in mind when reading this chapter. Let them percolate around the grey squishy between your ears and by the end you'll have answers — or, at least, the tools to find the answers.

1. What's your hero's goal?
2. What are you going to do to stop her from getting it?

Specificity

If you want to nurture your glorious web of connectivity, your conflict needs to have a level of specificity. It should be specific to both the hero and the villain to get them invested in fighting each other. It needs to *mean* something to them both equally. It should also be linked to their values and heightened by their emotions. But to really hammer the nail in the connectivity coffin you need to connect your conflict to the theme. For example, in *G.I. Jane* the major theme was female power. This is why much of the conflict was based on sexism and reducing her power, and her fight was triumphing as a powerful woman. It's all connected.

Types of Conflict

I like to break things down to the most basic units. Einstein is famed for saying that if you can't explain it to a six-year-old, you don't really understand it yourself. He's undoubtedly right.

Conflict can be broken down into three parts:

Macro conflict - These are large scale world wars, society against the hero, often found in dystopian novels as the 'final' villain that needs defeating. But this could be any war that spans more than just the hero. It could cross states, history, natural forces, the law, races and more.

For example, the faction system that categorizes every citizen in the *Divergent* series by Veronica Roth, or the man-killing Triffid plants in *The Day of The Triffids* by John Wyndham.

Micro conflict - This is a more interpersonal form of conflict — the battles the hero has with personal relationships, for example, between lovers, friends, family, colleagues and enemies.

In *Me Before You* by Jojo Moyes, the entire plot is based on a micro conflict. Will has a motorcycle accident that leaves him with a desire to end his life. Until Lou rolls into his world and tries to change his mind. Their desires: Lou's love for him, and his desire to die, smash into each other as they are in direct opposition.

Inner conflict - This is the smallest unit of conflict as it's internal only to the hero. It's the conflict the hero has with his own flaws, emotions and values. While it's the most isolated conflict, it's usually the most heart-wrenching as it's the conflict closest to the reader — particularly if you write in closer points of view like first person or third person limited.

Game of Thrones by George R.R. Martin is rife with inner conflict. One of Martin's specialties is giving characters conflicting values and loyalties. Jamie Lannister (known as the Kingslayer) killed the very king he swore to protect. Jamie even goes so far as to spell out the turmoil he's in:

> "So many vows... they make you swear and swear. Defend the king. Obey the king. Keep his secrets. Do his bidding. Your life for his. But obey your father. Love your sister. Protect the innocent. Defend the weak. Respect the gods. Obey the laws. It's too much. No matter what you do, you're forsaking one vow or the other." Jamie Lannister in *Clash of Kings* by George R.R. Martin.

In the same series, Theon Greyjoy is torn between his blood family and the adopted family that brought him up. Likewise, Brienne has a bizarre habit of putting honor before everything — including reason. She will follow her oaths even when logic and reason dictate that she shouldn't.

Balancing Conflict

As cheesy as it sounds, balance is the key to life. You know what's boring? Monotony. Even conflict in all its drama-fueled gossipy awesomeness can be boring if it's the same drama throughout a novel. Conflict is best served layered... like cake.

I like cake.

I also like conflict.

And I'm sure your readers will love both.

So layer your conflict like a Victoria sponge on steroids.

You can keep your reader's interest by layering different types of conflict on top of each other throughout your story. Or use multiple forms of the same type of conflict. But remember: balance is key. Too much, and it's confusing. Too little, and it's boring.

> **Example:** In *The Hunger Games* by Suzanne Collins there are multiple layers of conflict.
>
> Inner conflict from her torn feelings between Peeta and Gale.
>
> Micro-conflict that presents as physical fighting against the other tributes.
>
> Macro-conflict between her (and the people of the Districts) and the Capitol in the form of President Snow.

While layering conflict builds depth to your story (and occasionally your world-building), there is a big 'but' attached to the layers. It's important to remember that while all conflict builds pace, and layering it creates depth, it's the inner conflict that forms the best connection with the reader. And that's essential to keep the reader reading and growing their empathy for the hero.

> "Our tragedy today is general and universal physical fear so long sustained by now that we can even bear it. There are no longer problems of the spirit. There is only the question: When will I be blown up? Because of this, the young man or woman writing today has forgotten the problems of the human heart in conflict with itself which alone can make good writing because

only that is worth writing about, worth the agony and the sweat.
He must learn them again." William Faulkner, 1950, *Nobel Prize
for Literature speech.*

Conflict and Flaws

Conflict could, in theory, be about an infinite number of
topics. But the cleverest conflicts are designed to make the hero
confront his flaw. It's that moment where I reach across the table
to grasp my web of connectivity diagram and grin at you with a
glint in my eye. If you connect conflict to the theme, to your
protagonist's flaw, you get a web of bookish, reader-hooking
connectivity.

I mentioned the Disney movie *Planes* earlier. Dusty (the
protagonist's) major flaw is that he's afraid of heights. To win the
final race (the major conflict), Dusty must confront his flaw
directly. The only way he can win is to fly above the clouds and
go higher than he's ever been before, thus forcing him to face his
flaw and overcome it to achieve his goal.

Conflict and Theme

While you might have multiple conflicts in your novel, your
major conflict should be linked to your book's theme. It should
be the very expression of your moral or thematic question. Naturally, sledgehammering your reader around the face with it might
not be the best approach, but crafting it in a subtle way makes it
more like a gentle stroke to the cheek.

In *The Matrix* one of the core themes is the question of fate vs
free will: what free will is, whether we (humans) deserve it, and
whether it exists.

During the film, there are dozens of expressions of the theme
fate vs free will, although I'll only cover three main ones now. But
the point is these expressions of theme create conflict for Neo.

1. The world itself is constructed in two halves: the real world (what's left of it) represents free will and what having free will has done — destroyed the Earth, creating this hellish dystopian world — and the machine world, where everything is predetermined and 'fated' by machines.

2. Morpheus poses the first and most fundamental fate vs free will question to Neo by giving him the choice of a red pill or a blue pill. This produces inner conflict for Neo. Morpheus makes it clear to Neo that if he takes the red pill he will leave the comfort and protection of his 'known' life forever.

3. The final battle in the series of Matrix films poses the exact same conflict: fate vs free will. Neo was created inside the Matrix. Arguably he is fated to die to bring the destruction of the Matrix and, yet, he still has the choice of whether to go into battle or not. This produces yet more inner conflict linked to the theme. He goes, obviously, and the final battle is between man and machine a literal expression of the two halves of the world — fate vs free will — in a battle to decide which will conquer the other.

So How Can You Create Conflict?

I couldn't possibly list all the ways to create conflict here. Well, I could... but it would take forever and someone who's more of a word nerd than me is bound to come up with another one. So, I won't. Instead, here are a few ways you can build conflict under each overarching type:

Inner Conflict

Wounds

Old wounds serve to create all three forms of conflict. Many wars are started because of a disagreement between two people in power. I liken a wound to a soul scar. Ask yourself: what scars in your hero's past would make him fight for justice? Were his family murdered? Did he experience torture? Or maybe he failed to save his little sister and now the person that caused her death has come back into his life. soul scars impact a person's life. They're the kind thing a man goes to war over, which is why they create conflict.

Fears

There are a million fears a person can feel — spiders, heights, candy floss... But they can severely impact a protagonist's life. They could stop them applying for the big job they wanted, prevent them leaping off the bridge into the water to save their sibling. A protagonist's fear is a form of test. It makes the protagonist decide how important their goals and desires are. Can they face their fear to achieve their goal? It's the ultimate question. How much do you want it? Are you willing to face your fear to get it?

Love

The age-old war cause. Philosophers will tell you that love is the only thing worth fighting for. It certainly causes enough strife for characters. Love is fraught with doubt, self-consciousness and uncertainty. Falling in love makes you vulnerable, and that in itself is enough to create conflict in a character's psyche. The yearning for the other person butts up against the terrifying need to trust another person and give yourself to them. It's why you see the yo-yo'ing in romance novels as the couples try and fail to come together before the story's climax.

Values

Value conflict is one of my favorite forms of conflict. Values reveal our deepest held beliefs, and that often tells you a lot about a person. It's like slicing someone open and spreading their insides out like peanut butter and jelly on toast.

Values are fiercely held beliefs because they're integral to a person's sense of self. That's why when another character challenges them (like a villain or an antagonist) it creates excellent conflict. But you don't need another character to conflict against your protagonist's values. Your hero can do that by himself quite easily. I've already mentioned a *Game of Thrones* example (Ned Stark) who suffers with inner turmoil when the King asks for help. His loyalty demands he help but his wisdom tells him not to.

Micro Conflict

Family

Family. That beautiful rose covered in thorns. I love my family dearly... in small doses. I'm sure they'll forgive me for saying that. There's something universal about the love-hate relationship we have with our families. We'd slay our sibling's enemies, donate kidneys to our parents and just as quickly punch our brother in the gut when Dad wasn't looking... Just me? Oh, behave yourself. You know it's true. Families are a cesspit of conflict. It doesn't matter who you are; everyone's family is as nutty as everyone else's. And there's always a sordid secret buried about that trampy cousin or the odd aunt who kept a locked room that stunk like decaying flesh... Nobody needs those secrets revealing. Conflict arises when your character's values are put to the test. Is blood thicker than water? Do you protect your murderous aunt or do you value justice more than family?

However, it doesn't need to be life-altering conflict like murder. In *Bridget Jones's Diary*, her family wants her to date Mark Darcy, who she thinks is a Christmas-jumper-wearing plank. Mini conflicts are equally crucial to ratcheting up the tension and doubt, which drive pace.

Secrets

Secrets are pesky little things. Most commonly, they create conflict at the inner and micro levels. They can be put to good use at the micro level if the secret being kept impacts someone else in the hero's life. Heroes have a habit of thinking they're protecting someone by not telling them the secret. But, in reality, the opposite is often true. This kind of secret creates an inner conflict for the hero. They will then make mistakes and tell lies, trying to hide the original secret, producing even more inner turmoil over what the best course of action is.

Competition

Competitiveness — that secret sin we all profess not to have. Liars. All of you. Deep down we're wired to want to win. It's science. And if you're not competitive, then tough luck bitches. It's survival of the fittest. Darwin said so.

Macro Conflict

Macro conflict is like rolling out the big guns of world-ending conflict, instead of focusing on people and inner battles the characters have. This type of conflict can span worlds and generations. It also makes it a less tangible form of conflict — often framed as the big bad society with no face.

The Society or Government

This is typically found in dystopian, fantasy, science fiction, literary fiction or any story not set in contemporary society. There's usually an element of reality twisted to make a philosophical or moral point about a dysfunction in our world. These dysfunctions are an excellent source of conflict because, however the world is shaped, these governments and societies make life more difficult. They create separation between rich and poor, or skilled and unskilled or any other division. This inequality creates unfairness and hardship for huge swathes of humanity, which, ultimately, create my favorite type of character: rebels. For examples, think of *Day of The Triffids* by John Wyndham (one of my all-time favorite books), *1984* by George Orwell or *The Handmaid's Tale* by Margaret Atwood.

When a society or government device is used (and particularly in dystopian novels) it usually creates environmental and setting pressure. By that I mean that the physical environment a character is in becomes harder to survive in, thus creating a struggle and the possibility of conflict. In these settings, the basics needs of a human are compromised.

Maslow's Hierarchy of Needs

We interrupt this transmission to discuss something super awesome: Maslow's Hierarchy of Needs.

Maslow, an infamous psychologist, is famed for having created the hierarchy of needs in 1954. In dystopian, or other literature settings for that matter, one of the easiest way to create conflict is to restrict one of the lower more basic needs: food, water, oxygen, sleep and shelter. They are essential to life, and when you don't have them *you die*. Sounds dramatic, right? Well, that's why it creates conflict and characters will fight for them.

Of course, you can create conflict using the higher needs too, although the higher you go, the more personal the conflict is likely to be. Self-actualization is an internal battle to achieve your personal potential. It is influenced less by external factors and more by personal grit and determination. Self-actualization is in the name: it only affects the 'self', whereas basic needs like food and water are a global need and affect billions.

The lower the need, the more global the conflict. The higher the need, the more internal the conflict.

Religion

In the same way that values are extremely close to a person's sense of identity, so is religion. Many wars fought throughout history have been over religious conflicts. I won't get into a religious debate in this book. Suffice to say, religions — like values — are fiercely held. And this, when challenged, can escalate to conflict. Secondly, like society and government, religions have their own set of rules and law and, no matter the context, be it school, work or society, rules always get broken, and that leads to tension and conflict.

Power Struggles

I'm going to be philosophical and possibly controversial for a minute. Power is recognized as desirable. It's accepted by readers worldwide as a realistic cause for conflict: your villain wants power to do things. But what's often missing is the reason why. We've talked at length about why 'why' is so important, and that's no less true of a villain (or hero) pursuing power. There should be a reason, whether it's to create armies, control a sector of society or seek revenge. But even they aren't the *real* reason one goes after power. It comes back to the theme but also your personal philosophy (as the author). Why, at the core of a desire for power, do you think a person will fight for it?

Me? I think power is freedom. If you have enough power, you don't have to conform or adhere to any rules or laws. You're free to do as you please, be who you truly want to be. No more suppression, inequality or strife. As an author, you need to decide what the why is behind not just power conflicts, but all the conflicts. What will the thing being fought over give to your characters? More often than not, it will come back to Maslow's Hierarchy of Needs.

Impossible Odds

They're impossible for a reason. It's impossibly difficult to make the perilous journey to retrieve specific items (*Indiana Jones*), beat Apollo Creed (*Rocky* movie), or beat Johnny Lawrence (*Karate Kid*). Anything that's difficult creates conflict for several reasons. Two of the most popular reasons are because decisions are required over how to achieve the goal. The concept of impossible odds, when broken down, is really about winning something, whether that's power, respect or a Kung Fu cup.

Impossible odds often arise in brutal training regimes, too. Like G.I. Jane, who spends most of the film in a hardcore Navy Seals training ground. Almost all of the film's conflict occurs during her training because of power struggles, sexism and the desire for respect. More recently, Arya Stark from *Game of Thrones* goes through brutal training with the Faceless Man. She's beaten and temporarily blinded to succeed in her training.

From success comes disaster

I love anything that twists the expected into something unexpected. Turning what your hero thought would be a success on its head is an easy way to do this. For example, in *Frankenstein* by Mary Shelley, Victor creates Frankenstein. However, instead of being happy and overjoyed, he's actually sickened by his creation.

Jurassic World is another example of this, I mean, really? Bring back the man-eating, world-destroying dinosaurs, and what? Hope for the best? Phssst. That was never going to be a good idea, was it?

Emotion

"The most pivotal moments in people's lives revolve around emotions. Emotions make powerful stories." Brandon Stanton, author and photographer.

Emotions drive humans. We feel our way through life,

hurting and loving, caring and hating. It's the age-old adage head over heart — or is it heart over head? In either case, what we do when our emotions butt up against someone else's can cause problems. When you love something, you fight to the death over it. Therein lies your conflict. But it's not just love that creates conflict. Jealousy can cause a person to do vile things too, as can hate and many other emotions.

If your conflict needs to crank up the pressure, add in some emotional tension. Make the scene/action/journey you're writing deeply important to your protagonist (or your villain). Emotion makes everything more intense.

Emotions are universal, and that's what makes emotive scenes so appealing to readers. We all know what it means to be resentful, or angry, and we've all had those first flutters of love. I said it in STEP 3, and I'm saying it again now: *emotions are the only universal language.*

Pinch of Salt, a Sprinkle of Pepper and Leave to Boil

Creating and layering conflict is one thing, but conflict is like a work of art — far too beautiful to be left unappreciated. It's a sculpture standing in a museum waiting to be touched and prodded. It *wants* to be touched. It *needs* to be touched. Poking conflict rattles it and riles it up until it bursts open and spills tension and pace from its loins. Okay, I'm getting carried away. Back on topic, Sacha. We've established that conflict should force your hero to face his flaw. The reason this is so important is that facing your flaws allows for growth. Why? Because it shows you new parts of yourself.

But in order to get your hero to face his flaw you need to build up the conflict to a ferocious level of tension. Just as with creating conflict, there are a multitude of ways in which you can build it too. I'll give just a few here.

Doubt

Doubt is one of my favorite techniques to build conflict. Your readers see your story world through your hero's eyes, like hero-tinted glasses. What your hero feels, your reader feels. Therefore, when the hero expresses doubt, the reader is unsettled and unsure of the beliefs they may have built in the earlier parts of your story. Earlier, I used the Matrix as an example. Continuing with that film, Neo's biggest period of doubt comes after the Oracle tells him that he is not 'The One', making him face a deep fear that he is just an ordinary no-one who will let Morpheus and everyone else down. It casts doubt over who 'The One' is (for both Neo and the respective audience), and we're all left questioning whether or not Morpheus can find the right 'One' in time to save humanity.

Doubting other characters

Continuing on from self-doubt is doubt over other characters. *The Stepford Wives*, a satirical thriller by Ira Levin, is one of the best expressions of a hero doubting characters. When the hero questions another character, so too does the reader. The act of doubting another character creates tension, a feeling of unease as we (the reader) don't know the character's true motive. It's a great technique for making the reader keep flipping those pages until 3am on a work night.

In *The Stepford Wives*, Joanna, the protagonist, comes to the village and meets the wives of the local men. At first glance, the wives appear pleasant, perky, polite and submissive. Something anyone would mistake for friendliness. But as time progresses, and the wives continue to behave in the *exact* same way every time she meets them, she begins to feel unsettled. No one's that perky all the time, right? Doubt seeps into her mind over the wives' true nature. She questions how they can be so consistently happy. She's right, of course — the wives are robots. But until she discovers the truth, the doubt creates both inner conflict over whether Joanna is mad for questioning the other wives' behaviors and also the direct conflict between Joanna and the husbands who want to keep the secret of their robotic wives quiet.

Lies

> "Only enemies speak the truth; friends and lovers lie endlessly, caught in the web of duty." The Man in Black, Stephen King, *The Gunslinger*.

Lies are gorgeous little poison chalices. We've already covered the major form of literary lie — the lie your hero believes. But there are two other forms of lie: lies the hero tells and lies the hero is told. There are dozens of ways to craft mistruths for your heroes. And they don't all have to be huge life-changing lies, like in *Ender's Game* by Orson Scott Card. The lie is revealed in the climax when Ender discovers he is not actually playing a game like he's been led to believe, but is committing mass genocide.

Or smaller lies

Villains often use the truth as a weapon. Characters (including the hero) lie to protect other characters. That means the villain can manipulate the deception to his advantage. If the truth is a secret, then someone doesn't want it getting out, which means it's also a weapon. A good villain will use that fact to create threats or control and manipulate the hero into doing things he doesn't want to, and this creates conflict.

Example: *The Hunger Games* by Suzanne Collins. President Snow makes a point of telling Katniss that he will never lie to her, which he sticks too rigidly. And despite his warped mindset, that makes him trustworthy. This is why, when Snow reminds Katniss of the fact he's never lied, she knows that Alma Coin sent the parachutes which killed her sister, leading Katniss to kill Alma.

Example: *Once Upon A Time*, the TV series. Rumpelstiltskin also known as Rumple/The Dark One is a master of manipulation, using careful words and phrases to make deals that he would then manipulate to his liking. For example, The Evil Queen asks Rumple to frame Mary Margaret for Kathryn's murder. Except when The Evil Queen makes the agreement she asks for something 'tragic' to happen to Kathryn. So instead of killing Kathryn, Rumpel merely abducts her.

Misunderstandings and assumptions

Misunderstandings are another excellent tool for driving conflict because they often lead a character to believe something that either drives her further away from her goal, further away from another character or becomes hurtful to her emotionally. Vivian from the movie *Legally Blonde* catches Callaghan (a senior lawyer) flirting with Elle (a young student) and assumes that Elle is using her good looks to get ahead when, in fact, the opposite is true, although this doesn't come to light for Vivian until later in the story.

Hero Sacrifice — What It Really Means

I like a little hero torture, so shoot me: I'm a hardened villain sympathizer. But what's not always clear is what we mean when we say your hero needs to suffer for the win. Do we mean physical injuries and wounds? Sure, sometimes. Do we mean psychological torture and trauma? If it fits your story, why not? I've also known the concept to be implemented through the sacrifice of a hero's life, limb or all manner of other things.

But none of those really capture the essence of what's meant by 'your hero needs to sacrifice for the win'. What we — meaning me and all of the literary geekettes who care to have an opinion — usually mean is that the hero needs to give up a part of herself to win. The part is the flaw. The hero has to say goodbye to whatever flaw-shaped comfort blanket they had and sacrifice a piece of themselves in a heroic flaw-burning ritual with meditative chakra incense, mini blue-dyed party sausages, flaw-balloons, retro cheese-and-pineapple on sticks and halo-cake (yes, I mentioned cake again, shh). Or forget the party, but recognize that it's hard for anyone to truly overcome a flaw. Not only does it take strength and courage; you have to say goodbye to a part of yourself to overcome your weakness.

Up the ante, baby

Keep raising the stakes by adding in other elements to the conflict, whether it be more emotion or time pressure. Upping the ante creates tension, and that drives pace. Or maybe isolate your hero from all his allies and resources. Make the situation look hopeless. Repeatedly bring the antagonist into contact with the hero in tense situations.

STEP 7 CRAFTING CONFLICT SUMMARY

- The existence of a goal + prevention of the goal being achieved = conflict. Or even more simply: create a goal and stop the goal coming to fruition.
- Conflict should be specific to both the hero and villain in order to get them to invest in fighting each other.
- **Macro conflicts** are large scale world wars — society against the hero.
- **Micro conflicts** are more interpersonal as a form of conflict — the battles the hero has with personal relationships.
- **Inner conflicts** are the smallest unit of conflict as it's internal only to the hero. It's the conflict the hero has over his own flaws, emotions and values.
- Layer conflict to keep pace and raise the tension and emotion. Vary the type of conflict when layering.
- Link conflict to your hero's flaw and your book's theme.
- Remember Maslow's Hierarchy of Needs. The higher up you go, the more internal the conflict. The lower more basic the need is, the more global the conflict.

- Add doubt, lies and misunderstandings to make the conflict more acute.
- At its core, hero sacrifice really means the hero sacrificing a part of her inner self in order to become whole and unflawed.

Questions to Think about

1. What's your hero's goal?
2. What are you going to do to stop him getting it?

STEP 8 CLICHÉS VS TROPES

Clichéd villain spotting ought to be an Olympic sport. They're so common it's frankly painful. But spotting clichéd heroes is different. It's harder to identify a heroic cliché because heroes are universal and cover a much broader range of possibility.

But what exactly is a cliché and how is it different from a trope?

Clichés are words, phrases, expressions or scenes that have been overused to the point they've become predictable and unoriginal.

Classic examples include:

- 'Objection' used in a court scene when the prosecutor is losing
- A priest marrying a couple and saying 'Does anyone object?' and the protagonist's true love busting into the church, having run the last mile to stop the wedding
- A villain or a witch with a 'muhahaha' laugh or a cackle
- 'They all lived happily ever after'
- 'And then I woke up and realized it was all a dream.' (If I read your book and it says this, I will burn it.) Clichés

are cheesy, rotten, stinkin', mold-covered fleapits. And I don't mean the good blue cheese kind of mold; I mean the powdery mildew kind that would make you gag if you swallowed it. Does that mean I'm saying don't use clichés? Yes. But also, no. Let me explain.

See, everything in moderation is fine. One cliché in your hero can be easily forgiven or masked. But only if the rest of the time, you have a well-rounded character with decent motives and depth.

Historical Context and Your Get-out-of-jail-free Card

Another quick note on clichés is that sometimes they're actually needed. Take gangsters. Today, a gangster puffing a cigar with a whiskey tumbler in hand, sat by an open fire is a cliché, but back in the 1920s and 1940s it wasn't. Clichés develop over time. If you're writing a story set in a particular historical or societal context, there will inevitably be some clichés you need to use in order to keep your story realistic.

Some classic cliché examples:

- The perfect hero with no faults, also known as Mary and Gary Stu. Nobody likes Mary and Gary. Don't invite them to play.
- Knights in shining armor are equally annoying.
- And, much as I hate to say it, the dashingly handsome, naturally muscled, don't-have-to-work-to-look-good type of hero is also clichéd.

How Do You Avoid Using Clichés?

Realism. That's how.

Ensuring your world, characters and wars are a realistic representation of humanity and the choices humanity makes is the fastest way to avoid creating clichés.

More specifically, ensure your characters have motives and justifications for their behaviors. Knowing the root cause (or the reason why) your character does something instantly creates meaning to their actions. That creates depth of character, which leads to realism. And that, dear writer, dispels the cliché.

If you write stories where good and evil are on opposite sides of the battlefield, then realistic portrayals of humans are even more vital. It's like oxygen to the lungs. If the line between black and white or good and evil is too clear-cut, it goes against our basic heuristics. As we grow and develop, that baby caricature of what's good or bad fills with shades of gray, and we no longer accept such simple explanations.

What this comes down to is creating real characters. Your hero is going to fuck up and make bad decisions because he is, like we are, fallible. If you create a picture-perfect hero who has no flaws and knows how to save the world from the start, you haven't got much of a story and you certainly haven't got a character arc for him to develop over.

People aren't all good or all bad. So don't make your constructs of good and evil purely good or purely evil either. It's not midnight here, Cinders. We all like raving until the wee hours, pen in hand, laptop on fire... and if you don't, what kind of unnatural morning monster are you? [1]

In summary, for the most part, clichés ought to be avoided, but there's another little literary device that shouldn't be: tropes.

What Are Tropes?

Tropes are reoccurring themes, concepts and patterns usually found embedded within genres. Tropes help you identify what genre you're reading. What separates a trope from a cliché is that a trope can be

*used over and over again, as long as it's told in a novel way each time
and it won't irritate your readers.*

Hero tropes are much easier to identify. A little ruffling through the top 100 books in your genre and you'll easily spot them. Tropes shift and change with fads and fandoms. Marissa Meyer's Lunar Chronicles was one of the seminal books in the resurgence of fairytale retellings.

The expectations of a reader picking up a book in that genre will differ to the expectations of someone picking up a crime novel. Expectations are important. If you're retelling a fairytale... you gotta *actually retell the fairytale.* Everything else around that is up for grabs: swap genders, swap locations, create a half-robotic Cinderella like Meyer if you really want. But the only way you get your reader to come back for more is by knowing what to give them. Give them the tropes they want and build a unique story around them.

Tropes move and change with societal trends and tastes. Find a new genre? You'll find new tropes. But, thankfully, tropes are relatively slow moving. Here's a challenge for you, whatever genre you write in. Go to Amazon and into the top 100 list. Pick five books: three from the top 20, one from the top 50 and one from the top 100. Read the books. See if you can identify at least half a dozen similarities in what will all be unique stories. Tropes are the patterns and maps we should follow in a genre to please our readers.

When you read the list of trope examples below, try and reel off half a dozen books in the relevant genre that uses them, and I bet each story you think of is completely different.

Some Classic Trope Examples:

Young Adult Tropes

- Orphan protagonist or distant parents

- Love triangles
- A graduation ceremony

Fantasy

- The chosen one
- The one magical sword/potion/device that will save the world and is conveniently difficult to locate
- Prophecy

Crime

- A dead body discovered at the start of a novel
- A crime fighting detective overly dedicated to the job
- A maverick detective
- A murderer either arrested or killed at the end of the book
- Serial killers

Romance Tropes

- Boy meets girl
- Enemies to lovers
- Forbidden lovers
- Matchmaker
- Societal class divide between love interests
- Happy ever after endings

One of the best online resources for writers wanting to study patterns in literature, film, TV and basically any other form of consumable media is TV tropes https://tvtropes.org. If you're after examples or explanations, I highly recommend it. Be warned, though: while most spoilers are hidden (and only revealed with a click), some spoilers do occasionally appear on their site.

Non-clichéd but Still Equally Irritating Nuggets to Avoid

Clichés are annoying, but they aren't the only rookie mistake you should avoid when creating your hero. And before you send me angry emails about how your hero has aspects of the below, and you've sold a gazillion books... hush now, my wordsmithing babes. Remember 'the rules' chapter at the start of this book. All rules can be broken, except the ones that can't...

Here are some non-clichéd but still painful character quirks to avoid.

Fishwife whiny-hero syndrome: No-one likes a whiny nag at the best of times, least of all a whingebag protagonist. There are limited occasions when you can craft a woe-is-me character and get away with it. 99.8% of the time your audience will scream *Suck it up princess, you're the hero.*

Herosplaining: There's a modern turn of phrase 'mansplaining' which refers to the occasion when a man explains something to a woman in a condescending way. I'm fully coining the term herosplaining as a new word.

Heroes don't need to explain the following:

- The book's theme
- A metaphor within your book
- Their revelation or epiphany
- Their feelings

The explanation for any of the above, should be inherent through the action, dialogue and descriptive thoughts and feelings the hero has. Don't let your hero be a teacher with a cane at the board. Fiction is meant to be enjoyed in the peaceful heaven of a fine wine, a candlelit hot tub and... I lost my train of thought. Anyway, fiction readers don't come to be taught. That's what non-fiction is for.

Offensive mistakes: I'm going to be serious for a moment and say this exactly how it is. One of the most popular steps in *13 Steps To Evil* is the step dedicated to mental health. I wrote it because I was sick of how many villains are characterized with mental health issues as the cause of their villainy. Um, no. Mental health is an extremely serious topic, as are many other topics that writers choose to write about. It's a good thing that writers want to talk about and use fiction to dig into these topics. But what's not cool is when an author doesn't do their research. Two things happen:

1. The mental health disorder (or other topics like abuse, rape, etc.) isn't always portrayed accurately.
2. It leads to myths, misconceptions and stigmatizing of a sector of society.

Please don't think I'm saying this to make anyone feel bad. I'm not. And I don't want anyone to shy away from these topics; it's important that they're written about. But if you are going to cover them, then it's only fair to do the right thing and research the subject matter properly.

STEP 8 CLICHÉS VS TROPES SUMMARY

- Clichés are words, phrases, expressions or scenes that have been overused to the point they've become predictable and unoriginal. Examples include: 'And then I woke up and realized it was all a dream' or 'objection' used in a court scene when the prosecutor is losing.
- Tropes are the patterns and maps we must follow in a genre to please our readers. Examples include a maverick cop, boy meets girl and the chosen one.
- Sometimes clichés are actually needed, particularly in the case of historical context.
- Avoid clichés by having realistic motives, reasons why characters do the things they do and avoid black and white explanations of both good and evil.
- Don't herosplain. Just don't.
- Do your research on topics that could easily cause offense or marginalize a sector of society.

Questions to think about

1. Name three clichés and three tropes from your genre.
2. Think about your own hero and story. Have you used any clichés or tropes?

STEP 9 START WITH BANG, BANG, KAPOW

Writing advice tells you to start in the middle of the action. But when they say 'middle of the action', they don't mean it literally. The start of a novel is a fine art. Mix a cracking first line with a hook or question that pulls the reader through the rest of the novel. Add a dash of protagonist who's interesting, and you're partway there. I'm sweating even thinking about it. It's hard. Like trying-to-create-a-Michelin-starred-meal-when-you're-a-fifteen-year-old-apprentice-high-on-shrooms hard.

Here's What Starting with Action Doesn't Mean

It doesn't mean blowing shit up and launching into epic battle scenes with no explanation.

What it Does Mean

Think of your reader as a date. You wouldn't turn up on your first date, slide into the seat next to her, grin with your newly whitened teeth and slip your eager hand between her legs. That's going to earn you a broken nose or worse. And your book? Well, the reader's going to drop it faster than your date can drop a right hook.

So, what do you need to do? If we boil it down to the simplest parts, then three key things:

1. Establish your protagonist's 'normal world'
2. Tell the reader what the hero wants
3. Show (or imply) what the stakes are to the reader (which is, of course, predicated on what the hero wants)

There's probably going to be a boatload of you tutting and waving balled fists at me for saying you only need to do those three things. And sure, I get that there's a million other things you need to nail in your first chapter – a hook, making the reader care, setting the tone, including the theme, etc – but trust me, when you distill it down, if all you do is the above three things, you'll nail the rest anyway.

Prepare yourself. I'm about to whip out my favorite phrase like it's retro night and I'm big-fish-little-fishing it around the dancefloor.

It's all about the web of connectivity.

If you convey the protagonist's goal and the stakes surrounding it, the theme should be inherent. When combined, the goal and stakes are your magical reader-catching fishing hook. Together, they should give you a question, which reels your reader in until they get it answered. And that question generates enough initial care for your reader to keep turning those pages until the rest of the story can lull her into a reading binge long after the bat babies get tired.

Establishing the Normal World

Establishing the normal world has two aspects to it:

1. Establishing what the 'world' itself is like
2. Establishing what the hero is like in it

Change Is Predicated on Stability

Stay with me. I know that sounds like a contradiction, and it sort of is, but the reason you need to establish the above two points is because you can't send a hero on an adventure (where he will change radically) if the reader doesn't know what he's changing from.

Understandably, if your novel is set in our world there will be less world-building to establish. But in genres like fantasy, science fiction and dystopian, it's even more important to lay out the rules of the world, but without baseball batting your reader around the face with it. It's no good having your hero say 'oh I can't go to Hogwarts because I'm human'. That's preachy. No-one likes being preached at. Don't preach at your readers. It's bad for sales.

But How Do You Establish the World Without 'telling'?

Easy.

Your reader experiences your book world through your hero. They understand the rules and your society through the action your hero takes and the experiences she has in your story.

For example, everyone in my life knows not to talk to me unless it's 11 am or I've had two coffees. They've experienced the other side of morning-me and learned when not to talk to me.

If your hero experiences your world naturally through the course of your story and his interactions with other characters, it will allow your reader to immerse themselves fully in your world, without being yanked out to have the five laws of Hogwarts and muggle magic shouted at them. Strike a balance rather than over-loading your reader with world-building. The reader doesn't have to know the ins and outs of your royal hierarchy (unless it's relevant). If it's not relevant then you're information dumping. Avoid it like the plague, or herpes, whichever one you dislike more.

Allow your reader to dip her elegantly polished toe in the water, wading in tiptoed step by tiptoed step. Seduce them, woo them like the Victorians – a slip of fabric over the wrist, a flash of ankle. Let your reader discover parts of your world building at the same time your hero discovers them: that's when it's relevant, and not before.

Let me give you a couple of examples:

Example 1: *Delirium* by Lauren Oliver - a Dystopian novel.

"It has been sixty-four years since the president and the Consortium identified love as a disease, and forty-three since the scientists perfected a cure. Everyone else in my family has had the procedure already. My older sister, Rachel, has been disease free for nine years now. She's been safe from love for so long, she says she can't even remember its symptoms. I'm scheduled to have my procedure in exactly ninety-five days, on September 3. My birthday." Delirium by Lauren Oliver, pg. 1.

Granted, this opening scene is a little on the preachy 'telling' side. However, it's all in context. The protagonist is considering her future and her big birthday. As a result, she's explaining what procedure she has to undergo. From her sister's experiences, and her talk of love being a disease, we infer that scientists found a cure for love and that's what the procedure is. It also tells us that procedure is 'normal' for her world.

Example 2: *Divergent* by Veronica Roth

"There is one mirror in my house. It is behind a sliding panel in the hallway upstairs. Our faction allows me to stand in front of it on the second day of every third month, the day my mother cuts my hair." *Divergent* by Veronica Roth, pg.1.

This example is far less telling and much more showing. A simple scene – that simplicity is a clue to the world. Tris tells us that her house only has one mirror (again, another clue to her world) and that her 'faction' has rules that she must abide by. We know her world is dystopian because the rules are so different to ours. I mean, who only has one mirror in their house AND ONLY LOOKS AT IT ONCE EVERY OTHER MONTH. Think of the bed hair, people. The way the protagonist describes the length of time over which the habitual haircut happens tells us that this is a 'normal' ritual for their world.

Who Is the Hero Anyway?

And so to the second part of establishing normal. Let's be efficient and kill two birds with one stone.

At the start of this chapter I noted the three key things you need to do in your opening:

1. Establish the normal world
2. Tell the reader what the hero wants
3. Lay down the stakes

We've done the first. But the second, I've always thought, is terribly phrased for writing advice because we don't really mean *tell* the reader what the hero wants. After all, we're not supposed to *tell* the reader anything. The first lesson we learn as we crawl into the light from our word-mother's loins is 'show don't tell'. What we actually mean is *imply*. You need to imply the hero's goal.

Imagine a protagonist (a stable boy) talking to another stable boy about the Grand National while picking out a horse hoof and wistfully watching the champion jockeys train.

Bet you can guess his goal. I didn't tell you his dream, but the reader can be pretty certain, even in that short image, that the protagonist's goal is to someday be on one of those horses, racing with the best. You don't need to tell because creating an image with description and action implicitly shows the reader the hero's goal.

The last two key points, identifying desire and the stakes, are intricately linked. And the efficiency bird they kill? If you know what a person desires, and the stakes they're up against, I'd say you're fairly well acquainted with the 'normal' hero too.

Goal Specificity

Vague goals won't cut it. In fact, vague anything isn't going to cut it in your novel. Your protagonist's goal should be specific enough the reader can easily identify it. Michael Hauge in *Screenplays That Sell* argues that there are five types of specific goal:

Win - For example, winning that horse race I mentioned earlier, or winning the heart of a lover, or winning a battle against the lord of darkness, or Rocky winning the fight against Apollo.

Stop - Well, stop the bad guy! But it could be stopping a bomb from going off as in the *Speed* movies, or stopping the Terminator from killing John's mother, Sarah Connor. Or every James Bond film ever.

Escape - Of course, it doesn't have to be a prison as in the case of Andy Dufresne in *The Shawshank Redemption*. It could be escaping a husband, or a job, or a room like Jack and M, in *Room* by Emma Donoghue, or some big-brother-style reality like Truman in *The Truman Show*.

Deliver - This could be all manner of things from money in a gangster film to the Bible in *The Book of Eli*, where Eli must traverse an apocalyptical world and deliver the only copy of the Bible left in existence.

Get - In the movie *The Italian Job*, Charlie Croker wants to get gold bullion. Lara Croft wants to find Pandora's box in *Tomb*

Raider. 'Get' is often found in adventure stories, as they are usually quests to find something.

Often, stories combine goals, like *The Matrix*, which combines **escape** (as in escaping the Matrix itself), and **stop** (as in stopping Agent Smith from getting to Zion and wiping out what's left of humanity.

Lay the Stakes like It's a Vampire Fest and You're the Only Human at the Party

It's vital you lay down the gauntlet for the reader in chapter one because the reader needs to know what it will cost the hero to reach his goal. And sure, your stakes will rise and fall and maybe even change as your story progresses, but for the love of all things literary, make sure you whip out some kind of a stake in the early chapters.

Continuing with our earlier examples, Roth establishes the initial stake on page 2.

"Tomorrow at the Choosing Ceremony, I will decide on a faction; I will decide the rest of my life; I will decide to stay with my family or abandon them." *Divergent*, Veronica Roth, p.2.

Note how Roth doesn't bash the reader round the chops with the stake. She lets the hero infer the stakes through actions: Tris making a life-changing decision. Pretty substantial stakes, if you ask me.

Maybe you write crime, and a dead body or four show up – stakes laid: solve the crime before the killer strikes again. Or maybe you're a romance novelist, and the heroine's husband abandons her on the day she gets made redundant – stakes identified: find a way to support herself before her life totally falls apart.

Notes on Herosplaining and Exposition

Let's delve into the detail of why herosplaining is hideous and should be outlawed. Herosplaining and information dumping are siblings. Here's an example. Jeremy and Cal are long-term BFFs (Best Friends for Life for the acronym haters). Let's look at a little scene between Jeremy and Cal. What we (the readers) don't need, is the author *telling* us that Jeremy is Cal's best friend. Show the reader through their interactions.

Information dump example:

Fourteen-year-old Jeremy sauntered into the canteen and sat next to Cal who was also fourteen. Jeremy was Cal's best friend, they'd been friends since kindergarten. They met on their very first lunch break. Jeremy sat next to Cal just as the rather skinny lunch lady slopped a dollop of spagbol over their plates. Both of them pushed their plates away at the exact same time, after that, they were inseparable.

"Afternoon, Squire," Jeremy says.

Non-information dump example:

Jeremy sauntered into the canteen, his lips pressed into a thin grin. His eyebrows dipped over his glinting eyes as he caught sight of Cal. It was an expression Cal had come to love and loathe in equal measure.

"Afternoon, Squire," Jeremy said fist bumping Cal and plonking himself on the bench next to him.

"What are you planning Jeremy?" Cal asked.

"How'd you know?"

Cal rolled his eyes, "Same way I know you're hiding our pirate radio mic in your bag."

"I take '*Squire*' back. Hello, Sherlock."

Information dumps are easily identifiable because the information they give the reader isn't about action in the present story, but something from the past.

Typically, info dumps are about historical events, magical or societal constructs or anything that's remotely complicated in your protagonist's life (or your world's history). The dumps 'explain' behavior, action or relationships between characters. But 'explaining' is tantamount to telling, and every author in the history of written words knows the 'show don't tell rule'. If you don't, Google it.

Reasons Info Dumps Need to Go to the Sin Bin

Reason 1: Information dumps take the reader out of the protagonist's mind and out of the present action. I've established that readers experience the story through the feelings and perceptions of the hero. When we tell stories in real life, we don't naturally dump twenty years of personal history and life achievements to explain how your child achieved ten out of ten in their latest spelling test. Natural conversation is full of interruptions and tangents, so stories get told in snatches and glimpses.

Reason 2: They remind the reader they're reading. No one wants to be reminded of the calories they're consuming when shoveling secret eclairs into their mouth. You want the sickly-sweet pastry to coat your tonsils, and you want to be left in peace. Readers are the same. They want to escape into your novel, be fully immersed. If you dump info, you'll take that away. Don't take your reader's eclair away. It's mean.

Reason 3: It creates a fact-giving listicle utterly devoid of emotion instead of a gripping emotional rollercoaster of a plot. It also slows the pace. I mean, who wants to read a *War and Peace*-sized encyclopedia on the ins and outs of brick construction in the Far East quarter of quadrant seven? I was bored even writing that sentence, let alone the poor sod that needs to read it in a novel. If it's not relevant, KILL THAT DARLING. Sever it like a carotid artery in the muscled fingertips of James Bond's hands.

Who's in the Driving Seat?

Even though the hero is flawed at the start of the novel, and even though they are not 'actively engaged' in the story until they've picked up the mantle and accepted the call to action, **the hero should still drive the plot.** After all, if the hero refuses the call to action, it would make the mentor or ally wander in and encourage the hero to accept it.

The protagonist should be the most active character in your story and that should be the case right through to the finale. If you find your protagonist isn't the one driving your story through to the conclusion/climax, then they aren't your protagonist.

Your hero's worked through the obstacles in the story, so don't let someone else make the final blow on the villain. Imagine you're at work and you've worked for months or years on a project, and then someone else comes in at the eleventh hour to close it and inevitably take the credit. Nobody likes that person. That person's an asshole. Your hero needs to make the final blow because it should be the action in your story that requires the most risk or responsibility.

Example: *Harry Potter and the Philosopher's Stone* by J.K. Rowling. During the final climax of the story Harry, Ron and Hermione face a series of increasingly challenging spells woven by the school's professors to prevent people from entering the stone's secret chamber. Each spell got harder, but it wasn't until the final challenge that Harry had to face the biggest challenge of them all: Lord Voldemort.

Opening Gambit Clichés to Avoid

Although we've covered clichés more generally in Step 8, there's a couple more things to cover on clichéd beginnings.

I'm not here to tell you what you must and must not do, but even Edward Bulwer-Lytton is sick of hearing "it was a dark and stormy night." I've included a list of tired story starts below. That's not to say you *can't* use them, but I hope you're feeling super innovative when you do because the list is full of clichés for a reason. Your first line is your first impression, if you want my advice — which I'm assuming you do given you're reading this book. Mix it up. Avoid starting with these eye rolls:

- Dreams or waking up. (Just don't.)
- Weather (it's boring)
- Expository dialogue like 'As you heard, Joe..."
  Herosplaining is not cool
- Summaries (they're tantamount to info dumping)

STEP 9 START WITH BANG, BANG, KAPOW

- Starting with action doesn't mean blowing shit up and launching into epic battle scenes with no explanation.
- If we boil down the start of a novel to the simplest parts, then you need to do three key things:

1. Establish your protagonist's 'normal world'
2. Tell the reader what the hero wants
3. Show (or imply) what the stakes are to the reader (which is, of course, predicated on what the hero wants)

- Establishing the normal world has two aspects to it:

1. Establishing what the 'world' itself is like
2. Establishing what the hero is like in it

- Change is predicated on stability. You can't have a change if you don't know what you're changing from and to.
- Let your hero experience your world through the

natural course of your story and interactions with other characters. Doing that allows your reader to immerse themselves fully in your world.

- Only give world building information when it's relevant to the story.
- Don't herosplain or information dump. They're easily identifiable because they don't give the reader information about the present action in the story.

- Information dumps are bad because:

1. They take the reader out of the protagonist's mind and out of the present action.
2. They remind the reader they're reading
3. It strips your plot of emotion

- We don't really mean *tell* the reader what the hero wants. After all, we're not supposed to *tell* the reader anything. **You need to imply the hero's goal.**
- Types of goal: Stop, Get, Deliver, Win, Escape.
- The hero should be driving the plot, even when they're not actively engaged in the story.

Questions to Think about

1. What type of goal does your hero have?
2. How is your hero different from his or her normal self?

STEP 10 SPRINKLING THE UNICORN DUST - AKA THE HERO LENS

And so, we reach the final and most delicately nuanced chapter. The best bit about a cake is the icing (don't you dare say the sponge). It's so sweet it's like shooting up hallucinogenic sugar. In this book, we've thrown in our character ingredients: theme, arcs, traits, avoided the gone-off clichés and for flavor we've shaken and stirred motives and soul scars into the mix. What we've done is build a solid protagonist. Her motives stand up. The pace, conflict and arc she experiences evoke reader sympathy and bridge the connection from inky words to the reader's heart. And yet, there's still a little more...

There's still that little 'je ne sais quoi' missing. That something extra that makes your protagonist pop and sparkle enough she stands out of the slush pile. The something that makes your character the 1% – the Madonna of pop, the Elon Musk of Engineering, the Michael Phelps of... okay, you get it.

And here's where I whip out a cliché that makes my eyebrows twitch harder than a gorilla in a rave: *the devil is in the detail.* Eww, I feel dirty. But it's kinda true. The things that make us likable are the tiny nuanced variations. In some ways, this chapter is the pièce de résistance because it's where we look at how to go from the foundations of finger painting and Lego blocks to the master-piece of a Michelangelo.

You need to build your hero lens.

What in the Fudgebanging Collywomble Is a Hero Lens?

I'm so glad you asked.

Your hero is a bookish telescope, a strangely muscular funnel, a dashing mirror, a pair of protagonist-shaped glasses, a cape swishing magnifying glass... I'll stop now.

All those things are lenses in one form or another (and before you argue that a mirror isn't a lens, zip it Einstein, don't ruin the analogy). Your hero is the lens through which your reader experiences your novel. The mirror part? Well, that works too because we've already talked about how protagonists are a reflection of us, we see parts of ourselves in stories... You know, like a mirror. Just saying.

Everything the hero does, sees, feels and thinks, encloses your reader into a tiny literary lens. Nothing happens in your book unless your protagonist experiences it. Everything is channeled through her. She is the lens your reader looks through when reading your story. Readers want this lens. They covet it.

But that means your lens needs to be tinted in a slightly different color to everyone else's. It's time to ice that character cake and sprinkle on a bit of magical unicorn dust.

The Implicit Hero — the Hero's Voice

In researching this novel, I surveyed readers to find out what they found hardest when creating their heroes. The thing that came up the most often was how to get your reader to know your hero implicitly, without using expository dialogue or description. Another reader described it as wanting their audience to hear the hero's voice rather than their author voice. And yet another writer described the same problem as wanting to know how to express the hero as the hero wants. When there are too many traits and motivations to choose from, all the heroes sound the same.

I couldn't agree more. But motivations and traits are foundations. And the foundations of anything, whether it's a house or language or dancing, are the same. They're huge blocks on top of which you layer and build skills or bricks.

It's not the traits and motivations that make a hero unique; it's the way she embodies them. The expression of traits will impact how she experiences the world. For example, why can roast chicken smell thick and creamy to one identical twin and like sour flesh to the other?

The implicit hero shows the reader your story world through the five senses: how does the world look, sound, feel and taste to her? It's the expression of these senses that create the subtle nuances between one hero's lens and another's.

The lens is made up of four parts:

1. Actions
2. Thoughts
3. Dialogue
4. Feelings

These four are wholly unique to your character and your character's personality should be reflected through them.

But What Makes a Sparkly Unicorn a Sparkly Unicorn?

Because I'm all about full circles and connecting webs, I'm swinging back around to the Gestalt principle.

I'm a whole person. So are you. We're the product of our experiences, our upbringing and our traits. How I see the world is the culmination of all of those things and a little more – my conscious interpretation of the world, which will be different to yours. Let me ask you a question:

Is turquoise more blue or more green?

The answer is irrelevant, but what I can assure you is this: half of you reading that question said more green, the other half said more blue.

Understanding how and why it is you see things differently to everyone else helps you understand what makes your viewpoint unique. That's what you need to grasp for your protagonist. Often, we connect with each other because we either see the world through a similar lens, or our lenses are so different we learn something about ourselves from the other person. It's these similarities and differences that help us connect.

The way your protagonist describes her experiences – the metaphors and descriptor choices – tells the reader about their personality. It creates the nuances and quirks that separate one hero from another. It also demonstrates those traits in action.

An angry hero might see a town parade like this:

The villagers weave through the street brandishing placards like rifles. They're soldiers marching into their last battle. The war-drum beat of their feet grinds into my ears, rattling my teeth and making my blood boil.

But a depressed hero might see the same town parade like this:

They move like a current, each person flowing past the next. Supposedly united in their cause, but as they chant and sing for solidarity, it sounds like the melody of mourners. I see the tiny fractures, the gaps they leave between each other, the scattered looks, the fear of isolation. Each of them is drowning in a swelling crowd, and yet, despite the mass of bodies, they're all fighting alone.

In both of those examples, I haven't used either the word 'angry' or 'depressed' and yet those emotions are implicit in the paragraphs. Why? Because of the hero lens. Each protagonist experiences the same event. Yet they feel, hear and see different things.

How the character sees the world, how they feel or smell or taste, combined with their traits and experiences, creates distinctions between characters. Imbuing your hero's descriptions with their unique sense of personality will give your hero depth and make them sparkle on the page.

Here's an example in fiction, the main character in Melissa Albert's *The Hazel Wood*. Alice is an intense and curious girl who likes to tear the skin off the world just to see what's underneath. Here's a couple of examples of how Albert embodies her personality through her description:

"He sat up straighter, his eyes refocusing on mine. The serene smile inched back onto his face, but now that I'd seen beneath it, I could tell it wasn't a perfect fit." Melissa Albert, *The Hazel Wood*, p.98.

"But already the edges were rubbing off the memory's freshness. I could feel it degrading in my hands." Melissa Albert, *The Hazel Wood*, p.21.

Most characters don't think about the texture and the feeling of a memory or the fact that it degrades as time passes. But Alice does because she looks at the world in intense detail like she's unwrapping the layers of every character she meets.

Quirks Versus Habits

Often writers will turn to quirks and habits to make a hero seem different. I want to be clear on the difference between a character **habit** and a character **quirk**.

A habit is a routine movement, action or behavior often

done in a repeated pattern. It's automatic and something a reader would deem normal.

For example, pushing your glasses up, checking the doors locked before bed or always reading the newspaper in the morning.

A quirk is unique and idiosyncratic to your character; it's a deliberate behavior. Usually, it will stick out to your reader or other characters.

For example, in the movie *East is East*, one character, a young boy called Sajid, refuses to take his jacket off, EVER. He wears it rain, snow, sun or sleeping. This is a quirk because it's unusual and out of the norm.

One way to create a believable character quirk is to integrate it into your story. Rather than having the quirk as an add-on, give it a function in your novel, whether that's connected to a flaw, part of character growth or an obstacle.

Another handy trick is to have the quirk accentuating one of your hero's personality traits or flaws. Like Monica Geller from *Friends* with her cleaning habits.

Quirks typically help:

- define your character by distinguishing them from other characters
- show the reader the character's uniqueness rather than telling them
- create tension
- create conflict
- create a barrier or flaw for the hero to overcome

Spice Is Spicy, Quirk Is Quirky

Your taste buds are inevitably different to mine. I quite like to sweat while I eat my curry. My spouse on the other hand, curses the air blue when I sprinkle even the tiniest of pepper pinches into our lasagna. Readers are the same. Some want hardcore hero-in-your-face, smothered in oil, banter dropping their jaws. While others prefer the more demure and reluctant hero.

Wherever your preference lies, we all have our limits. While I might appreciate a hot curry, I don't want to sweat blood while I eat. There's only so much spice a regular girl (or reader) can take. It's better to use a handful of herbs and spices and savor the flavor than to blow your taste buds into the next century by trying to demolish a Phaal curry. It's the same for quirks and traits. It's better to give your hero one or two quirks and make the most out of those, than it is to have a loud gregarious hero with extreme charm, intense banter, blue hair and a toenail eating fetish. It's too much. It overpowers the flavor of the story and the reader loses sight of the hero's true personality. Subtle and nuanced quirks work more effectively and efficiently than an oil tanker full of them.

Making Memories

Despite living a short time, we meet tens of thousands of people throughout our lives. Yet when we're old and drooling, we only remember a small handful. It's not the loud garish ones who shout the loudest that we remember. It's the ones who had the greatest impact on us, for example:

- They changed us in some way – making us think differently or by giving us a realization about ourselves
- They made us feel something
- They surprised us
- We related to them because we saw part of ourselves in them

Let me give you a real-life example.

Travel is my second passion, so every spare penny I have goes on my next adventure. On one particular trip to Paris, I'd decided

I wanted to buy some macaroons. When in Paris... Rome? Moving on.

I'd been eyeing up a rather cute looking macaroon shop all weekend and decided to fill my sugary boots. The shopkeeper came to my assistance as I was visibly distressed by the extensive rainbow of biscuity delights. She asked me what I wanted. So, I started to order. I managed to order a couple: lemon, caramel, rose (obviously) but then I attempted to order a vanilla macaroon... This is how the conversation went:

Me- "Can I have a vanilla one please?"

Shopkeeper- "Non."

Me- "Huh?"

looks at an entire rack of vanilla macaroons

Me- "Sorry, umm, I meant one of those ones."*points at vanilla macaroons*

Shopkeeper- "Oui," she nods, indicating she understood which macaroon I meant.

I jab my finger at the vanilla macaroons again, (just to make sure... cause, I *really* want a vanilla macaroon).

Shopkeeper - "Non."

Me- "Um. Okay? Why?"

Shopkeeper- "They no good."

Me- "Riiiight?!"

I gave up and ordered some other flavors. But she found a permanent home in my memory as the shopkeeper who refused to sell her own goods. I won't forget her because what she did was unexpected. I mentioned the psychological heuristics we build as children in Step 3 — they help us 'know' fundamental things. Things like 'red' on the road means stop, or that girls have bits boys don't, and that chocolate is the food of gods.

My heuristics tell me that it is quite literally the shop owner's job to sell me her goods. When she refused to – and especially because she deemed her macaroons not good enough – it rocked my teeny tiny world.

Surprises catch a reader's attention. Going back to my previous point, that it's better to have one or two quirks than hundreds — the rest of the shopkeeper was perfectly normal. In fact, I couldn't even tell you what she looked like now. The only thing I remember is the quirk.

This technique is often used when a character's personality has been well established to indicate change or emotion/reaction. But it's just as useful for introducing characters and creating humor.

Using the Unexpected

The unexpected is one of the most powerful tools you have at your disposal as a writer. If readers know what to expect the entire way through your story, what would be the point of reading it? This tool is top-notch unicorn dust. Sprinkle that shit liberally.

It's also effective at describing character's appearances:

"You look like edges and thunderstorms. And I would not have it any other way." Roshani Chokshi, *The Star Touched Queen*, p.98.

Characters are rarely compared to weather. It was unexpected and that's why it caught my attention. The contrast between clouds, which are soft and fluffy (even if they are thunder ones), and the hardness of an edge, is so rich, and it's a unique description to that character. It's that character's lens.

Likewise, the unexpected can implicitly tell the reader about the protagonist's personality.

"Bleeding in three places, I watched her go, glad she knew I'd rather have retribution than comfort." Melissa Albert, *The Hazel Wood*, p.51.

Despite bleeding in three places, the protagonist happily watches her mother leave her. This is unexpected because society expects mothers to flock to protect their babies. It's especially shocking when the mother abandons her bleeding daughter not to seek help, but revenge. What is more telling is that the daughter approves of her mother seeking revenge for her. This tiny sentence tells the reader so much: the protagonist values retribution over comfort, she's tough enough to look after herself when injured and she got that attitude from her mother.

Juxtapositions

Juxtapositions are quite possibly my favorite literary device. A juxtaposition is defined by Dictionary.com as

> "An instance of placing close together or side by side, especially for comparison or contrast."

Juxtapositions aren't just used in description. You can weave them through emotion, dialogue, theme and action. Some of my favorite scenes contain juxtaposed emotions.

Juxtapositions and Emotion

The reason juxtapositions work with emotion is that humans are layered and complex beasts. Psychologically, we rarely feel just one thing. For example, when a loved one passes away after a long and traumatic illness most are desperately sad, but some will also feel relieved that their relative is no longer in pain and the trauma is over for everyone.

Replicating that mix of emotions in your characters adds depth to both the scene and the complexity of your protagonist (or other characters). It makes them seem real because that's what we do as people.

Rip Your Hero's Heart out and Smear It Across the Page

The key here is how you display those emotions. For humans, it's rare that we feel two strong or contradictory emotions openly. What tends to happen is that we display the stronger emotion (or the emotion we think is expected of us) openly. Then we hide the conflicting emotion by either suppressing it or keeping it to ourselves. But, more often than not, our actions and body language give us away, it's these clues you need to give the reader. Clues, subtlety and what's not said create the implicit hero. Think of the conflict as inner and outer emotions.

In the example I mentioned above – the loss of a loved one after a long traumatic illness – the outer emotion would be sadness and the inner emotion would be relief.

A juxtaposed emotive scene will have an 'obvious' central emotion. Usually, that's the more explosive ones like anger, sadness or hate. Simmering underneath will be the softer, more conflicted emotions like regret, relief or love.

To show both in a scene in a realistic way without 'telling', you need to keep the emotions separate. The more explosive 'outer' emotion should be shown through action and dialogue. The inner emotion should be shown through thought and body language.

For example, the relative standing by the side of their loved one's deathbed might burst into tears. But it's the subtle sag of their shoulders that tells you they're also feeling relief. The combination of those emotions isn't necessarily unique, but the way your hero expresses it will be – that's your hero's lens.

"My voice trailed off as the Darkling turned slowly to me, his slate eyes drifting to where my hand gripped his sleeve. I let go, but I wasn't giving up that easily." Leigh Bardugo, *Shadow and Bone*, p.46.

Alina feels fear at the Darkling's movement and stops what

she was doing, but her after thought is full of determination not to give up.

Juxtapositions in Description

The reason juxtapositions are so effective at describing people is because they evoke such strong imagery. That's never truer than when describing characters. Melissa Albert, author of *The Hazel Wood*, is a master at using juxtapositions for descriptive purposes.

> "Beneath the beauty and the charm and the sharp sparkle of her personality, she had a core of steel. She was like a blade wrapped in a bouquet of orchids. I hoped to god whoever took her made the mistake of underestimating her." Melissa Albert, *The Hazel Wood*, p.112

Albert pits beauty and charm, something often seen as soft, against 'sharp and steel'. It evokes such a clear picture of what this woman was like, especially when combined with the additional simile – which is also juxtaposed – comparing the character to a blade buried in orchids.

I'm not saying you have to litter your novels solely with juxtapositions for the rest of your linguistically descriptive career. Far from it. What I'm trying to do is demonstrate how studying and using different literary devices can bend and shape your hero's lens. Where one character (Alice) is intense and detailed, another character (Hermione) might be intelligent and mildly arrogant.

Become a Hoarder

In this final section, we're going to look at ways to strengthen your prose and, in doing so, enhance your ability to create unique hero lenses. But first, I want you to create a new habit.

Task: When you read, ensure you have a pack of Post-its with you, or shredded paper – something to mark the page. Depending on how willing you are to mark a book, a pencil would be handy too. When you read, try and pick out sentences and passages of description or dialogue that particularly attract your eye. If it attracts attention, there will be a reason, and hopefully not because they're rubbish! When you finish the novel, review all of the sentences that caught your eye and try to spot the patterns. Buried in there will be the hero's lens. Somewhere in the rhythm and pace of sentences, in the word choice and device usage, will be the mark of each character's lens.

The Action Lens

Action was the first aspect of the hero lens I noted earlier. Depending on what action your hero is taking, whether it's in a fight or a moment of perspective, the style of description will change.

For example, in a fight scene, movements and actions are typically speedy and violent. Your prose should reflect this. Shorter sentences create pace and push the reader through your story quicker. Cleaner language has the same effect. The fewer descriptive words there are, the faster your fight scene will be. Actions should be described physically in real terms rather than in metaphors and similes.

But a scene where your character is falling in love would be described differently. When someone falls in love, they pay attention to every tiny detail about the person they're falling for. They become more aware of their senses and the sensations their bodies are experiencing, which is synonymous with slow sentence structures filled with metaphors and similes.

Quick tip: Think about the action your characters take. Can you reflect that in the structure and composition of your prose?

Example: *The Star Touched Queen* by Roshani Chokshi

"His hands roamed over the threads, fingers flicking, yanking, snarled in strands that he pulled out in swift, merciless strokes like he was tearing throats instead of threads." Roshani Chokshi, *The Star Touched Queen*, p.173.

This is one long, luxurious sentence, and that length reflects the action the character is taking – pulling out long silky threads from a tapestry. But it also has an interesting simile comparison. Chokshi deepens the smooth, gentle imagery of thread pulling by comparing it to something violent, like tearing throats. This tells you (implicitly) about the hero's lens and her perception of the other character. The comparison to violence tells you (without saying it explicitly) that she is uneasy and distrusts the character.

Passages of Time and the Act of Change, Aka Before and After

If your hero changes through their character arc, then it's only natural to assume that their perspective changes too. Protagonists have epiphanies and realizations about different aspects of themselves as they reach the climax of their character arc. These realizations are profound enough to enable them to overcome their flaw. Surely, if the realization is powerful enough to do that, you can assume their 'perspective' or lens will warp and distort too. They will see and therefore describe the world and their experiences in a new light.

Example: *The Star Touched Queen* by Roshani Chokshi

"Her voice had lost none of its smoke-rasp, but where it was once husky and sultry, it was now like dragged-over stones. The darkest sense of triumph snuck into my heart." Roshani Chokshi, *The Star Touched Queen*, p.265.

This sentence shows the passing of time as the protagonist

compares what she saw in a character earlier to how her voice appears now. It also shows the degradation of the character she's describing. The fact the protagonist's feeling triumphant indicates how she's changed. What's not clear is whether the character was always like that, and it's only now the protagonist's changed that she can see the character for what they are, or if the character really has degraded. The point is the sentence reflects the change in the protagonist's lens.

Don't Be Afraid to Be Silent

The thing with protagonists is that they're always front and center. This means you can easily fall into the trap of thinking you need them to be noisy. But some of the most powerful conversations are silent.

Example: *The Hazel Wood* by Melissa Albert
"Her silence was louder than Harold's voice. It's her greatest power, though she never used it on me. She'll stare at you as you try to pull your thoughts together, to say something that'll reach her, but she'll never reach back. I've watched her pull things out of people—secrets, confessions, promises to let us stay an extra month—with her silence alone. She wields it like a weapon." Melissa Albert, *The Hazel Wood*, pp.26-27.

I adore this description for so many reasons. Firstly because it shows the power of silence, but also because of the way the protagonist (Alice) describes her mother. While Alice describes her mother's use of silence as a weapon, she also says 'she never used it on me'. That statement holds a level of implied arrogance. Alice thinks she's above her mother's ways, and deems herself better than everyone else, but it also gives her a blind spot.

"I knew it was coming, but the words still took a chunk out of me. I stayed very still when he said them, because I didn't know what else to do." Melissa Albert, *The Hazel Wood*, p.111

This is another example of how your protagonist might use silence as a powerful descriptor of both emotion and action. We've all experienced emotional overwhelm. Some of us scream and cry, others retreat into themselves to process emotion. Again, it's an example of how a hero's lens can vary and how actions can implicitly tell the reader so much.

STEP 10 SPRINKLING THE UNICORN DUST — AKA THE HERO LENS SUMMARY

- Everything the hero does, sees, feels and thinks encloses your reader into a tiny literary lens. Nothing happens in your book unless your protagonist experiences it. Everything is channeled through her. She is the lens your reader looks through when reading your story.

The lens is made up of four parts:
1. Actions
2. Thoughts
3. Dialogue
4. Feelings

- The way your protagonist describes her experiences – the metaphors and descriptor choices – tells the reader about their personality.
- Imbuing your hero's descriptions with their unique sense of personality will give your hero depth and make them sparkle on the page.
- **A habit is a routine movement, action or behavior**

often done in a repeated pattern. Usually, it's automatic. It's something that a reader would deem normal.

- **A quirk is more unique and idiosyncratic to your character, it's a deliberate behavior.** Usually, it will stick out to your reader or other characters.

Quirks typically help:

- define your character by distinguishing them from other characters
- show the reader a character's uniqueness rather than telling them
- create tension
- create conflict
- create a barrier or flaw for the hero to overcome

It's not the loud garish people we remember. Usually, it's the ones that have the largest impact on us, for example:

- Someone who changed us in some way – making us think differently, or by giving us a personal realization.
- Someone made us feel something.
- Someone who surprised us.
- Someone we related to because we saw part of ourselves in them.
- Doing something unexpected is one of the most powerful tools you have at your disposal as a writer.

- The reason juxtapositions are so effective at describing people is because they evoke such strong imagery.
- The more explosive 'outer' emotion should be shown through the action and dialogue. The inner emotion should be shown through thought and body language.

- A juxtaposed emotive scene will have an 'obvious' central emotion, usually, the more explosive of emotions, like anger, sadness or hate. Simmering underneath will be the softer more conflicted emotions like, regret, relief or love.
- If your hero changes through their character arc, then it's only natural to assume their perspective changes too. If the realization is powerful enough to change them as a person, it's natural to assume their 'perspective' or lens will warp and distort too. They will see and describe the world in a new light.

Questions to Think about

1. What quirk or habits does your hero have?
2. Have you used all elements of the hero lens in your story?

CONCLUSION

You did it. You stuck with my made-up words and bizarre analogies for an entire 45,000 words. I hope if you made it this far, you've learned a thing or two about creating a hero with a sprinkling of dust on his halo.

You should have understood that stories are more than the sum of their parts. Gestalt it, baby. Weave that web of connectivity and remember: your hero is the embodiment of your story. Most of the steps in here are the foundations, the bricks and mortar you need to put in place so you can layer your particular hero's lens over.

In the appendices there are lists galore, including positive and negative traits, soul scars and more.

If you're still nervous, don't be. Remember, rules are there to be broken and beauty — or maybe I mean heroism — is in the eye of the beholder. It's up to you to decide what your hero should look like, but I hope that you base your decision on what you've learned, as well as the tropes of your genre and market. Don't stop studying. Break down your favorite hero's structure and study it in forensic detail.

This is it. Congratulations on graduating Hero School. All you need to do now is chuck the hero ingredients in, mix them around and slide your novel in the oven. Bake for 80,000 words and voila.

You've got this.

Go forth, and bake ye a hero... and me a cake!

THANK YOU

Thank you for reading *10 Steps to Hero*. I hope you found it helpful as you created your hero.

If you liked the book and can spare a few minutes, I would be really grateful for a short review on the site from which you purchased the book. Reviews are invaluable to an author as it helps us gain visibility and provides the social proof we need to continue selling books.

If you would like to hear more about future publications or receive a checklist to help you create a villain, please sign up here.

https://sachablack.co.uk/newsletter

ACKNOWLEDGMENTS

I'm not sure why writing the second book in a genre is so brutal, but both of mine have been. Which is why I have a number of thank yous to give.

Thank you first to my wife for being patient with my creative ways, and for supporting me to follow my dream. For the thoughtful things you do, like researching laptop stands when my back is breaking. You'll get that Mercedes... I promise. Atlas, you are the reason I work every night, sneak words in corridors and coffee queues and constantly strive for more. One day, I will show you that it's possible to follow your dreams and succeed.

Thank you to my mum for filling my childhood with magical stories and moving libraries when I'd read everything in our local one. You gave me the key to imagination, and for that I'll always be grateful. Dad, thank you for your no-nonsense support and making believe I am capable of anything.

To my writing girls, Suzie, Helen and Lucy, we will succeed in literary world domination. One word, one sentence, one book at a time.

Allie Potts, my accountability partner, who on more than one occasion this year had to tell me to pull up my big girl panties and soldier on. You saved me from so many tantrums.

Adam Croft... Legend, occasional comedian, secret mentor, grammar Nazi, reluctant friend... your support means more than you'll ever know. Thank you.

To Dr. Amy Murphy (or possibly now Shennan) thank you for over a decade of friendship and being the nerdy shrink we all knew I'd never be. Your input and psychological fact checking is always deeply appreciated.

To the writers, bloggers, friends and readers who filled out my research survey and made this book possible, I am indebted.

Last, and most importantly, thank you to you, the readers, for taking the time to buy and read this book. I hope it's been helpful and I wish you every success in your writing career.

ABOUT THE AUTHOR

Sacha Black is a bestselling and competition winning author, rebel podcaster, speaker and casual rule breaker. She has five obsessions; words, expensive shoes, conspiracy theories, self-improvement, and breaking the rules. She also has the mind of a perpetual sixteen-year-old, only with slightly less drama and slightly more bills.

Sacha writes books about people with magical powers, sapphic books for teens, and other books about the art of writing. She lives in Cambridgeshire, England, with her wife and genius, giant of a son.

When she's not writing, she can be found laughing inappropriately loud, blogging, sniffing musty old books, fangirling film and TV soundtracks, or thinking up new ways to break the rules.

sachablack.co.uk/newsletter
www.sachablack.co.uk
sachablack@sachablack.co.uk

Image Credit @Lastmanphotography

instagram.com/sachablackauthor
bookbub.com/authors/sacha-black
facebook.com/sachablackauthor
twitter.com/sacha_black
amazon.com/author/sachablack

ALSO BY SACHA BLACK

The Better Writers Series

Sacha has a range of books for writers. If you want to improve your villains, your heroes or your prose, she's got you covered.

To improve your villains:

13 Steps to Evil: How to Craft a Superbad Villain

13 Steps to Evil: How to Craft a Superbad Villain Workbook

To improve your side characters:

8 Steps to Side Characters: How to Craft Supporting Roles with Intention, Purpose, and Power

8 Steps to Side Characters: How to Craft Supporting Roles with Intention, Purpose, and Power Workbook

To improve your prose:

The Anatomy of Prose: 12 Steps to Sensational Sentences

The Anatomy of Prose: 12 Steps to Sensational Sentences Workbook

FURTHER READING

Character development

- 13 Steps To Evil - How To Craft A Superbad Villain, by Sacha Black
- The Emotion Thesaurus by Angela Ackerman and Becca Puglisi
- The Negative Trait Thesaurus by Angela Ackerman and Becca Puglisi
- The Positive Trait Thesaurus by Angela Ackerman and Becca Puglisi
- Creating Character Arcs by K.M. Weiland
- The Writer's Guide to Character Traits, by Dr. Linda N. Edelstein

Studying Story Structure

- The Anatomy of Story by John Truby
- Writer's Journey: Mythic Structure for Writers by Christopher Vogler

- The Story Grid: What Good Editors Know by Shawn Coyne and Steven Pressfield
- Dan Wells lectures on the seven point plot plan https://www.youtube.com/playlist?list=PLC430F6A783A88697

Studying Screen Writing/Screen Structure

- Save The Cat by Blake Snyder
- Screen Plays That Sell by Michael Hauge

Negative Traits Listing			
Abrasive	Abrupt	Agonizing	Aggressive
Aimless	Airy	Aloof	Amoral
Angry	Anxious	Apathetic	Arbitrary
Argumentative	Arrogant	Artificial	Asocial
Assertive	Astigmatic	Authoritarian	Barbaric
Bewildered	Bizarre	Bland	Blunt
Boisterous	Brittle	Brutal	Business-like
Calculating	Callous	Cantankerous	Careless
Cautious	Charmless	Childish	Clumsy
Coarse	Cold	Colorless	Complacent
Complaintive	Compulsive	Conceited	Condemnatory
Confidential	Conformist	Conservative	Cowardly
Crafty	Crass	Crazy	Criminal
Critical	Crude	Cruel	Cynical
Decadent	Deceitful	Delicate	Demanding
Dependent	Desperate	Destructive	Devious
Difficult	Dirty	Disconcerting	Discontented
Discouraging	Dishonest	Disloyal	Disobedient
Disorderly	Disorganized	Disputatious	Disrespectful
Disruptive	Dissolute	Dissonant	Distractible
Disturbing	Dogmatic	Domineering	Dull
Easily Discouraged	Egocentric	Enervated	Envious
Erratic	Escapist	Excitable	Expedient
Extravagant	Extreme	Faithless	False
Fanatical	Fanciful	Fatalistic	Fawning
Fearful	Fickle	Fiery	Fixed
Flamboyant	Foolish	Forgetful	Fraudulent
Frightening	Frivolous	Gloomy	Graceless
Grand	Greedy	Grim	Gullible
Hateful	Haughty	Hedonistic	Hesitant
Hidebound	High-handed	Hostile	Ignorant
Imitative	Impatient	Imprudent	Impulsive
Inconsiderate	Incurious	Indecisive	Indulgent
Inert	Inhibited	Insecure	Insensitive
Insincere	Insulting	Intolerant	Irascible
Irrational	Irresponsible	Irritable	Lazy
Libidinous	Loquacious	Malicious	Mannered
Manner-less	Mawkish	Mealy-mouthed	Mechanical
Meddlesome	Melancholic	Meretricious	Messy
Miserable	Miserly	Misguided	Mistaken
Money-minded	Monstrous	Moody	Morbid
Muddle-headed	Naive	Narcissistic	Narrow

Negative Traits Listing			
Narrow-minded	Natty	Negativistic	Neglectful
Neurotic	Nihilistic	Obnoxious	Obsessive
Obvious	Odd	Offhand	One-dimensional
One-sided	Opinionated	Opportunistic	Oppressed
outrageous	Over-imaginative	Paranoid	Passive
Pedantic	Perverse	Petty	phlegmatic
Plodding	Pompous	Possessive	Power-hungry
Predatory	Prejudiced	Presumptuous	Pretentious
Prim	Procrastinating	Profligate	Provocative
Pugnacious	Puritanical	Quirky	Reactionary
Reactive	Regimental	Regretful	Repentant
Repressed	Resentful	Ridiculous	Rigid
Ritualistic	Rowdy	Ruined	Sadistic
Sanctimonious	Scheming	Scornful	Secretive
Sedentary	Selfish	Self-indulgent	Shallow
Short-sighted	Shy	Silly	Single-minded
Sloppy	Slow	Sly	Small-thinking
Softheaded	Sordid	Steely	Stiff
Strong-willed	Stupid	Submissive	Superficial
Superstitious	Tactless	Tasteless	Tense
Thievish	Thoughtless	Timid	Transparent
Treacherous	Trendy	Troublesome	Unappreciative
Uncaring	Uncharitable	Unconvincing	Uncooperative
Uncreative	Uncritical	Unctuous	Undisciplined
Unfriendly	Ungrateful	Unhealthy	Unimaginative
Unimpressive	Unlovable	Unmotivated	Unpolished
Unprincipled	Unrealistic	Unreflective	Unreliable
Unrestrained	Non-self-critical	Unstable	Vacuous
Vague	Venal	Venomous	Vindictive
Vulnerable	Weak	Weak-willed	Well-meaning
Willful	Wishful	Zany	

Positive Traits Listing			
Accessible	Active	Adaptable	Admirable
Adventurous	Agreeable	Alert	Allocentric
Amiable	Anticipative	Appreciative	Articulate
Aspiring	Athletic	Attractive	Balanced
Benevolent	Brilliant	Calm	Capable
Captivating	Caring	Challenging	Charismatic
Charming	Cheerful	Clean	Clear-headed
Clever	Colorful	Companion	Compassionate
Conciliatory	Confident	Conscientious	Considerate
Constant	Contemplative	Cooperative	Courageous
Courteous	Creative	Cultured	Curious
Daring	Debonair	Decent	Decisive
Dedicated	Deep	Dignified	Directed
Disciplined	Discreet	Dramatic	Dutiful
Dynamic	Earnest	Ebullient	Educated
Efficient	Elegant	Eloquent	Empathetic
Energetic	Enthusiastic	Exciting	Extraordinary
Fair	Faithful	Farsighted	Felicific
Firm	Flexible	Focused	Forceful
Forgiving	Forthright	Freethinking	Friendly
Fun-loving	Gallant	Generous	Gentle
Liberal	Genuine	Good-natured	Gracious
Hardworking	Healthy	Hearty	Helpful
Heroic	High-minded	Honest	Honorable
Humble	Humorous	Idealistic	Imaginative
Impressive	Incisive	Incorruptible	Independent
Individualistic	Innovative	Inoffensive	Insightful
Insouciant	Intelligent	Intuitive	Invulnerable
Kind	Knowledgeable	Leader	Leisurely
Logical	Lovable	Loyal	Lyrical
Magnanimous	Many-sided	Masculine (or feminine)	Mature
Methodical	Meticulous	Moderate	Modest
Multileveled	Neat	Non-authoritarian	Objective
Open	Optimistic	Orderly	Organized
Original	Painstaking	Passionate	Patient
Patriotic	Sane	Peaceful	Perceptive
Perfectionist	Personable	Persuasive	Planner
Playful	Polished	Popular	Practical
Precise	Principled	Profound	Protean
Protective	Providential	Prudent	Punctual
Purposeful	Rational	Realistic	Reflective

Positive Traits Listing			
Relaxed	Reliable	Resourceful	Respectful
Responsible	Reverential	Romantic	Rustic
Sage	Scholarly	Scrupulous	Secure
Selfless	Self-critical	Self-denying	Self-reliant
Self-sufficient	Sensitive	Sentimental	Seraphic
Serious	Sexy	Sharing	Shrewd
Simple	Skillful	Sober	Sociable
Solid	Sophisticated	Spontaneous	Sporting
Stable	Steadfast	Steady	Stoic
Strong	Studious	Suave	Subtle
Sweet	Sympathetic	Systematic	Tasteful
Teacher	Thorough	Tidy	Tolerant
Tractable	Trusting	Uncomplaining	understanding
undogmatic	Unfoolable	Upright	Urbane
Venturesome	Vivacious	Warm	Well-bred
Well-read	Well-rounded	Winning	Wise
Witty	Youthful		

Neutral Traits Listing			
Absentminded	Ambitious	Amusing	Artful
Ascetic	Authoritarian	Big-thinking	Boyish
Breezy	Business-like	Busy	Casual
Cerebral	Chummy	Circumspect	Competitive
Complex	Confidential	Contradictory	Crisp
Cute	Deceptive	Determined	Dominating
Dreamy	Droll	Dry	Earthy
Effeminate	Emotional	Enigmatic	Experimental
Familial	Folksy	Formal	Freewheeling
Frugal	Glamorous	Guileless	High-spirited
Hurried	Hypnotic	Iconoclastic	Idiosyncratic
Impassive	Impersonal	Impressionable	Intense
Invisible	Irreligious	Irreverent	Maternal
Mellow	Modern	Moralistic	Mystical
Neutral	Noncommittal	Non-competitive	Obedient
Old-fashioned	ordinary	outspoken	Paternalistic
Physical	Placid	Political	Predictable
Preoccupied	Private	Progressive	Proud
Pire	Questioning	Quiet	Religious
Reserved	Restrained	Retiring	Sarcastic
Self-conscious	Sensual	Skeptical	smooth
Soft	Solemn	Solitary	Stern
Stolid	Strict	Stubborn	Stylish
Subjective	Surprising	Soft	Stern
Stolid	Strict	Stubborn	Stylish
Subjective	Surprising	Tough	Unaggressive
Unambitious	Unceremonious	Unchanging	Undemanding
Unfathomable	Unhurried	Uninhibited	Unpatriotic
Unpredictable	Unreligious	Unsentimental	Whimsical

Positive Values			
Authenticity	Accountability	Achievement	Adventure
Attractiveness	Balance	Challenge	Clarity
Commitment	Communication	Compassion	Competitiveness
Competency	Confidence	Continuous learning or growth	Courage
Creativity	Curiosity	Dependability	Determination
Discipline	Efficiency	Enthusiasm	Ethics
Excellence	Fairness	Flexibility	Freedom
Friendship	Generosity	Happiness	Health
Honesty	Humor	Independence	Integrity
Justice	Kindness	Knowledge	Leadership
Love	Loyalty	Openness	Optimism
Pleasure	Persistence	Respect	Security
Self-respect	Spirituality	Stability	Strength
Success	Support	Trustworthiness	Vision
Wisdom			

Negative Values			
Anger / Rage	Anxiety	Bitterness	Condemnation
Criticizing others	Cynicism	Depression	Despair
Despondency	Discouraging	Disinterested	Failure
Fame	Fear	Frustration	Gloom
Greed	Guilt	Helplessness	Hostility
Humiliation	Jealousy	Judgmental	Illness
Inequality	Lethargy	Loneliness	Misery
Ostracism	Pessimism	Pleasure	Regret
Rejection	Resignation	Rigidity	Sadness
Self-doubt	Sorrow	Status	Suspicion
Withdrawal	Worry		

Soul Scars			
Saved someone's life	Survived a car crash	Lost a limb	Went to war
Failed to make it to a deathbed	Divorced	Abandoned by parents/ lover/ sibling	Rejected by loved ones
Unrequited love	Failed	Continuous failure	Failed exams
Had to care for a loved one long term	Neglected as a child	Terminal illness	Lied to
Being cheated on	Victim of crime	Surgery	Addiction
Raped	Miscarried	Death of a child	Toxic friendship
Fell out of or lost friends	Involved in a cult	Lost religious belief	Witnessed cruelty or crime and weren't able to help
Experienced a natural disaster	Tornado	Hurricane	Earthquake
Tsunami	Bullied	Abused by parents/spouse	Manipulated
Death of a loved one	Lied to about your parentage or familial line/heritage	Was adopted	Lon period of unemployment
Kidnapped	Crossed a moral line to survive	Broke the law for the right reason	Made redundant
Sacked	Period of mental illness	Depression	

NOTES

Step 3 Perfection Perfected

I. Please note, no offence was meant to anyone who is actually a psychopath. But, you know... emotional apathy and all.

Step 8 Clichés vs Tropes

I. You should know, at least 30% of this book was written at 5am. I'm a hypocrite. What can I say? My black heart just prefers midnight. No matter how productive I am at the crack of dawn, damnit, I'll always love being a night owl.

Printed in Great Britain
by Amazon